VIETNAM TEN YEARS AFTER

edited by ROBERT EMMET LONG

THE REFERENCE SHELF

Volume 58 Number 2

THE H. W. WILSON COMPANY

New York   1986

THE REFERENCE SHELF

The books in this series contain reprints of articles, excerpts from books, and addresses on current issues and social trends in the United States and other countries. There are six separately bound numbers in each volume, all of which are generally published in the same calendar year. One number is a collection of recent speeches; each of the others is devoted to a single subject and gives background information and discussion from various points of view, concluding with a comprehensive bibliography. Books in the series may be purchased individually or on subscription.

Library of Congress Cataloging in Publication Data

Main entry under title:

Vietnam ten years after.

(The Reference shelf ; v. 58, no. 2)
Bibliography: p.
1. Vietnamese Conflict, 1961–1975—Addresses, essays, lectures.   2. Vietnam—History—1975-   —Addresses, essays, lectures.   3. Vietnam—Description and travel— 1975-   —Addresses, essays, lectures.   I. Long, Robert Emmet.   II. Series.
DS557.7.V5665   1986   959.704'4   86–1642
ISBN 0-8242-0724-6

Printed in the United States of America

THE
REFERENCE
SHELF

CONTENTS

IV. Ten Years Later: Retrospective Views
    of the Vietnam War

PREFACE

Although the Vietnam war concluded ten years ago, with the fall of Saigon in 1975, there is a sense in which it never ended. The experience continues to be felt by millions of Americans: by the families of those who died in Vietnam, by those who served in the war and returned home to be as much shunned as honored, and by those who resisted the draft or demonstrated against the war until the nation became an ideological battlefield. At the highest levels of government the defeat suffered in Indochina continues to have a traumatic impact. The self-doubt and self-questioning that followed Vietnam has not been fully dispelled. The notion of an invincible United States was called into question, and policy makers no longer assume that American troops can intervene effectively against Communist expansionism anywhere in the world.

Since the end of the war a debate has been taking place about its meaning and implications. A Vietnam literature has grown up in novels, plays, films, and television documentaries; and in the forum of magazines and journals many aspects of the war are discussed, often passionately and with wide differences of opinion and viewpoint. It can be seen more clearly today that the Marxist utopia envisioned by the North Vietnamese in their "liberation" of the South has not been realized. The regime in Vietnam is markedly repressive, with "reeducation camps" for thousands suspected of ideological deviation. A steady stream of refugees, including a vast number of "boat people," have fled from Vietnam since the war, creating a new immigrant population in the United States and other countries. The economy of Vietnam has been crippled by a complicated and archaic bureaucracy and by the mobilization of a huge standing army—the fourth largest in the world—which has invaded and taken over the territory of its neighbors, Laos and Cambodia. At the same time, the United States has begun to honor its Vietnam veterans belatedly and to reassess its role in world affairs.

Section I of this volume reprints articles in a variety of national magazines about the state of Vietnam today, while section II looks at the issue of Vietnam's occupation of Cambodia. Section III focuses on the United States—its Vietnam veterans and the fate of POWs and MIAs. Section IV reprints articles that debate the question of American involvement in Indochina and the future direction of U. S. foreign policy.

The editor is indebted to the authors and publishers who have granted permission to reprint the materials in this compilation. Special thanks are due to Ellen Morin and the Fulton Public Library staff, and to the staff of Penfield Library, State University of New York at Oswego.

ROBERT EMMET LONG

March 1986

THE LEGACY OF WAR: VIETNAM TODAY

EDITOR'S INTRODUCTION

However successful the North Vietnamese may have been in carrying out their long war against the United States, they have little to boast of in their management of the country since the war's end. Their attempt to apply Communist central planning has resulted in very significant failures. War-ravaged industry has not been rebuilt; unemployment is at an all-time high; and the rate of inflation is as high as 100 percent annually, making Vietnam one of the poorest countries in Southeast Asia. The crippled state of their economy is due in part to their maintenance of a huge standing army, which patrols the border with China and occupies Cambodia, now called Kampuchea. Economic collapse has been staved off by the infusion of 2 billion dollars into the country annually from the Soviet Union, in return for which the Soviets have been given access to the American-built military base at Cam Ranh Bay. The irony of this situation is that, having fought to expel one major power, the Vietnamese now find themselves dependent on another.

The introductory articles in this section, written by Robert Kaylor and reprinted from *U. S. News & World Report,* survey conditions in Vietnam's capital cities, Hanoi and Saigon, now renamed Ho Chi Minh City. As Kaylor points out, Hanoi is a city of decaying buildings and a political leadership of aged men whose attitude toward almost every issue has been rigid and doctrinaire. An atmosphere of growing disillusionment, he writes, can be sensed in post-war Hanoi as large numbers of Vietnamese, feeling balked in their attempt to find a better life, wait for legal permission to leave the country. In the article on Saigon, Kaylor stresses the prevalence of the black market as a means of negotiating survival, and of the many homeless and unemployed people, some of whom had been sent to "new economic zones" only to return to the city as drifters, living on relatives. "'Where Is My Father?,'" by Melinda Beck, reprinted in *Newsweek,* treats another under-class of people, the Amerasian children fathered by American ser-vicemen during the war and left behind, unwanted, and scorned for their black or Caucasian features. Although some are being re-settled in the U. S. under the Orderly Departure Program, the rate of departure has been painfully slow. A final article in this section, an excerpt from Craig R. Whitney's personal narrative in the *New York Times Magazine,* describes a land where people feel that they have no future. What strikes him chiefly about Saigon is an unhappy regimentation and a yearning on the part of many to leave the country.

HANOI STILL ACHES A DECADE AFTER VICTORY[1]

HO CHI MINH CITY

Ten years after the Communist military triumph in Vietnam, this impoverished country and its long-suffering people face a bleak future that cannot be disguised by huge anniversary celebra-tions stage-managed by the regime.

For more than a month, crowds of people in big cities and ru-ral hamlets have dutifully turned out to mark the April 30, 1975, surrender of Saigon, now called Ho Chi Minh City, by waving paper flags, cheering wartime heroes and applauding the Marxist revolution.

But among most Vietnamese—victors and defeated alike—the anniversary will come and go without changing the harsh realities of daily life. Even amid the festivities there are clear signs of deep economic decline and growing popular disillusionment. Among them:

• Industrial output in both the northern and southern halves of a now nominally unified nation continues to lag behind 1975, when war still raged.

[1]Reprint of an article by Robert Kaylor, staff writer. *U. S. News & World Report.* 98:60-62. My. 6, '85. Copyright © 1985 by *U. S. News & World Report.* Reprinted by permission.

- Food production consistently falls below government targets, leaving Vietnam's 60 million people with less to eat than during the long years of fighting France, the U.S. and one another.
- At least 1 million Vietnamese are awaiting legal permission under an "orderly departure" program to join 1.5 million people who already have fled the country. Hundreds more escape by boat every month.
- National survival depends almost completely on aid from the Soviet Union. There is no hard currency to meet 600 million dollars in foreign loans now due or 6 billion that someday must be paid to overseas creditors.

Vietnam's current plight is in stark contrast to expectations of peace and prosperity that were widespread even among non-Communists a decade ago. The future looks even more dismal in comparison with impressive growth in other countries of Southeast Asia.

"Any nation in this part of the world that goes into the 21st century a poor man isn't going to stand a chance," predicts a Hanoi-based Asian diplomat.

A trip through Vietnam's decaying big cities and picture-postcard countryside dramatizes how zealously the country's leaders from the North are celebrating their victory over the U.S. and South Vietnam 10 years ago—and how little they have accomplished since.

Ho Chi Minh City, renamed in honor of the founding father of Indo-Chinese Communism, has been given a physical and ideological scrubbing to mark the anniversary of the humiliating American withdrawal and the surrender of a stunned South's government.

Public buildings that had gone without maintenance for years were repainted. Signs went up around the city hailing victories at Ban Me Thuot, Hue and Da Nang that enabled North Vietnamese tanks and troops to roll on to Saigon in far less time than the Communists themselves had ever anticipated.

Children spirited away. The police rounded up Amerasian children—offspring of American servicemen and local women—and shipped them to undisclosed sites outside the city. Many of those youngsters have been waiting for years to go to the U.S. under a program bogged down in local delays.

Also taken into custody were dissenters and potential "destabilizers" who might mar the organized celebrations or attract the interest of more than 200 foreign journalists who flocked to Vietnam to cover the anniversary.

Officials tried to put a more Marxist stamp on the local economy with a crash campaign to bring free-market traders—60 percent of Ho Chi Minh City's merchants—into state co-ops. Decrees fixing prices and limiting profits were imposed to curb inflation, now running at an annual rate of 50 percent.

Even sellers of smuggled television sets and other electronic wares were put into stalls bearing neat blue-and-white signs proclaiming participation in government organizations.

But little has changed despite threats that economic offenders will be sentenced to forced labor. Black-market exchange rates have jumped by 20 percent since January 1. Joining the underground commerce are corrupt Communist officials from the North who cannot live on salaries equal to about $4 a month in real purchasing power.

"When they impose new rules, people find new ways around them," says one black-market trader who typifies a common South Vietnamese attitude.

Though the black market thrives, much of the economy is foundering. Exorbitant taxes, to discourage private enterprise, have forced owners of many stores and other businesses to close. Others stay open under "joint venture" rules that give the regime a dominant voice in operations and earnings.

Officials admit that 200,000 of Ho Chi Minh City's 2.5 million or more people are unemployed. Every year, residents pay stiff customs duties on more than 400,000 parcels sent here by relatives abroad. That often is the only way to obtain items such as medicine, clothing or even ball point pens.

People live under the constant shadow of a secret-police system that encourages schoolchildren to inform on parents for "antirevolutionary activities" such as hoarding or planning to migrate.

One South Vietnamese who chose to stay here and take his chances with the new regime characterizes life today as a mixture of hope, fear and uncertainty.

North grimmer. Whatever old Saigon's woes are, the North's conditions are grimmer. Hanoi's once graceful French colonial buildings are decaying. Few motor vehicles are on the potholed streets. Senior Communist aides often must get to work by bicycle. Factories still bear bombing scars and are further crippled by power shortages.

The infamous "Hanoi Hilton" that once housed U.S. prisoners of war now is an ordinary jail. It dominates a downtown street, its tan-colored walls topped by broken glass and electrified wire.

Outside the capital, many roads are merely rutted tracks. The 1,000-mile rail trip between Hanoi and Ho Chi Minh City takes three days and three nights, with trains in the North pulled by antiquated steam engines. Construction equipment is so scarce that armies of peasants in conical hats dig out silted irrigation ditches by hand during monsoon rains or form human chains to transport bricks for road repairs.

In contrast to those in the South, people in the North cannot leave for foreign countries under the United Nations–run orderly departure program and have only slim chances of fleeing illegally by boat. Instead, they join a long waiting list to be included among about 50,000 "guest workers" in the Soviet Union or other nations in Eastern Europe. The jobs often involve hard labor and require paying part of every worker's salary to the Vietnamese government. Even so, says a diplomat in Hanoi, "their conditions abroad are better than they have at home."

Despite strict surveillance by uniformed and secret police, more Vietnamese are expressing disillusionment about the failures and shortcomings of the past 10 years.

A visiting Soviet technician recently related, with considerable surprise, a comment of a Communist official in the south: "Ho Chi Minh told us in 1955 that there would be a time of trouble, that the liberation soldiers would come and that there would be gradual improvement. We had the trouble, and the soldiers came, but we are still waiting for improvement."

Doubts even are surfacing in Hanoi, where few in the past dared criticize the regime. "It's been 10 years, but there is no peace," one Vietnamese said to a visitor. "Now there is fighting with China. It always continues."

Asian and Western experts cite three closely intertwined reasons for Vietnam's troubles. One is the costly occupation of neighboring Kampuchea. Another is the burden of the world's third-largest military machine, behind only the Soviet Union's and China's.

The bottom line. Most important of all is the inability or unwillingness of a small group of stubborn Communist leaders to modify the tactics that they used to win the war to meet the very different demands of peace and economic development.

There are few indications that any of those factors will be altered in the foreseeable future either by internal decision or by outside pressure.

The 6-year-old occupation of Kampuchea, for instance, has triggered a punishing war and continuing conflict with China, the chief supporter of the Pnompenh regime toppled by Hanoi. It also is responsible for a U.S.-led economic embargo, which has shut off Western aid and technology that are vital for rebuilding war-shattered industries and transportation facilities.

However, efforts to force Vietnam into a political settlement in Kampuchea have been futile. "They can stay there as long as they want," acknowledges one diplomat. "It all depends on how long they want to remain isolated and behind the rest of Asia."

To occupy Kampuchea and protect a vulnerable 930-mile-long frontier with China, Vietnam maintains an Army of 1 million plus large numbers of part-time troops. Military spending takes almost one third of the national budget.

Most of the 2 billion dollars' worth of U.S. weapons captured in 1975 are now unserviceable. So instead of selling rubber, coffee and other commodities for badly needed hard currency, Vietnam must barter them to the Soviet Union for military equipment. Hanoi's army in Kampuchea is plagued by a slow but steady drain of desertions, an unheard of situation in earlier fighting. Southern youths eagerly volunteer for three years of hard labor on state farms to get an exemption from military service.

The continued occupation of Kampuchea, formerly known as Cambodia, also is at the core of Hanoi's quarrel with the United States. Washington is demanding a complete withdrawal and greater cooperation in the search for missing American war dead in return for diplomatic relations that could open the way for large-scale Western aid.

Some non-Communist nations that have diplomatic relations with Hanoi have urged greater flexibility toward the U.S., arguing that this would be a small price for an end or relaxation of the present economic embargo.

Hanoi's answer. The Vietnamese bent slightly in April by allowing a U.S. military team to examine an American air-crash site. But Hanoi gives no sign of leaving Kampuchea and now says that the initial search for war dead requires that the United States give something in exchange—with no guarantees of future Vietnamese cooperation.

Hanoi's Foreign Minister Nguyen Co Thac describes the approval for Americans to visit one crash site as "a special case to whet their appetite."

Specialists in Vietnamese affairs are highly doubtful that there will be any significant change in Hanoi's rigid, doctrinaire approach to almost every foreign and domestic issue as long as the country's aging but still powerful leaders remain in office.

Hard-line core. Prime Minister Pham Van Dong, party chief Le Duan and other top officials all are in their 70s. All achieved power during decades of war and are wedded to a system of facing down crises by refusing to budge an inch.

Even the majority of the younger members of the 15-man ruling Communist Party Politburo—men well into their 60s—are considered hard-liners with little taste for compromises or reforms.

A decade after Saigon's collapse, many battlefields that provided bloody images for a generation of Americans are again lush with greenery, showing few signs of the wartime devastation.

But this country and its people carry deep wounds. Until the leaders in Hanoi permit the wounds to heal, Vietnam is doomed to remain isolated, strife-ridden and impoverished in ways that few people could have foreseen a decade ago.

A DECADE AFTER SAIGON'S FALL, A PAINFUL PEACE[2]

Ho Chi Minh City

Travel the length of South Vietnam a decade after it was over-run by Communist armies from the North and you step in and out of eerie time warps.

Still clearly evident in palm-shaded villages and the crowded, pungent markets of Ho Chi Minh City—as Saigon now is called—are the corruption, consumer goods and other familiar holdovers of a freewheeling American-dominated era that ended abruptly in April, 1975, when the Communists poured into Saigon.

Equally apparent, however, are the regimented politics, Marxist economics and officially fostered mistrust that Communist overlords are resolved to impose on a reluctant, stubborn South.

For a reporter who covered Vietnam during the 1970s, a 25-day trip through this land of extraordinary beauty and bitter political quarrels discloses change on every side. Yet it also emphasizes how different the two halves of this nation still are—and how long they probably will remain that way.

Most immediately striking on city streets, along country roads and in Vietnamese homes is the visual evidence of economic decline and austerity in this once vibrant, reasonably prosperous country.

Much of what was independent South Vietnam still is richer than the victorious North. However, Southerners all across the economic spectrum are markedly worse off than they were before the departure of a half-million freespending GI's and the end of the massive U.S. aid program.

Communist leaders frequently proclaim that most of the ragged wartime beggars are gone from the streets of Saigon, Da

[2]Reprint of an article by Robert Kaylor, staff writer. *U. S. News & World Report.* 98:45–47. Ja. 21, '85. Copyright © 1985 by *U. S. News & World Report.* Reprinted by permission.

Nang and other cities. That is true. But the main reason for this is the even earlier disappearance of almost everybody from whom to beg.

Lack of foreign exchange to buy petroleum and spare parts has cleared away old Saigon's nerve-jangling traffic jams. The noisy, exhaust-fouled streets where Army trucks and Honda motor scooters once jostled for space now are quiet byways occupied mainly by bicycles and pedicabs. Most of the few cars still running are occupied by privileged government or Communist Party officials.

The downtown sidewalks that throbbed far into the night to the beat of rock and soul music pouring from open doorways of profitable—often disreputable—girlie bars now are deserted and dark soon after sunset. Many streetlights are turned off permanently to save scarce and expensive electric power.

Nevertheless, strong reminders of the old days and old ways are still easy to find just around a good many corners, often to the frustration of new rulers trying to impose new lifestyles.

Black-market stalls that once were crammed with goods from U.S. post exchanges still operate openly in many of their old locations. Today, the portable television sets and stereo tape recorders are smuggled in on ships from Singapore, Hong Kong and other non-Communist ports. Customers include Soviet-bloc tourists and technicians, plus a sprinkling of Vietnamese.

Prices are high. A pair of Asian-made blue jeans, one of the most popular items, cost 4,000 dong—about $15 at black-market rates but equal to three months' salary for an average factory worker. Many customers are farmers, who can buy a Japanese TV set from the proceeds of selling four pigs on the now legally sanctioned open market.

Marital festivities. During December, traditionally the favorite month for Vietnamese weddings, Ho Chi Minh City's only nightclub—once the Rex Hotel officers' billet familiar to thousands of Americans—was booked solid every night for parties hosted by bridal couples with the cash to entertain lavishly.

Most of the brides and bridegrooms wore expensive Western attire in an unspoken challenge to official efforts to root out both ostentation and the remnants of American culture.

On one recent afternoon, a Communist official was leading young men and women through rifle drills in a downtown park decorated with Marxist posters and a picture of the late North Vietnamese leader Ho Chi Minh. On a nearby side street, Western rock music blared from a house where young couples danced enthusiastically and waved to a foreigner passing by.

Masses in the city's Roman Catholic cathedral attract overflow crowds of worshipers despite official support of atheism and the arrest of a number of religious leaders.

Less visible than economic decline—but no less real—is another kind of repression. Now absent is the danger of being jailed or tortured by secret police for espousing leftist ideas, a threat ever present under the previous regime.

"Re-education" camps. The old system has been replaced by one that is perhaps even worse: Grim "re-education" camps where many with past ties to the U.S. are held. Fear of the government's informers is strong and pervasive enough to generate suspicion even within tightly knit Vietnamese families.

There never has been an accurate tally of the total number of South Vietnamese sent to re-education camps in the chaotic months following the fall of Saigon in 1975. Some escaped or eventually were released to survive as best they could under a regime that considers them social and political outcasts. But many—estimates run as high as 40,000—former military officers, Saigon government officials and onetime political leaders still are held under harsh conditions, while Washington and Hanoi argue over terms for permitting them to enter the U.S.

Last fall, the Reagan administration proposed that up to 10,000 re-education-camp inmates and their dependents be allowed into the U.S. on the same basis as other Indo-Chinese refugees. But authorities in Hanoi are insisting on formal U.S. pledges to restrict émigrés' anti-Vietnam political activity in America before approving any releases.

Making fear work. One of Hanoi's few successes in the South has been creation of a widespread atmosphere of fear and mistrust. A government decree makes it illegal for ordinary citizens to talk with foreigners—including allies such as the Soviets—unless it is a necessary part of their jobs. Propaganda in schools and on television regularly urges youngsters to tell police if their parents engage in "antirevolutionary activity" such as hoarding valuables or planning to flee the country.

Despite restrictions, Vietnamese often feel safer talking to Westerners than to their friends and neighbors. They assume that foreigners will not betray them. "Anyone can be an informer," explains a Ho Chi Minh City resident. "You do not dare speak about the government, even to your friends."

A young woman puts it this way: "Distrust makes the city a lonely place. The war was not good. But Saigon was much happier then."

For the new regime, the informer network is a key element in maintaining tight political control. Loose talk among Vietnamese, who have never been good at keeping secrets, reportedly made it relatively easy for security police to round up what it claimed was a spy ring of former military officers and refugees who infiltrated the city last year with Chinese-supplied arms.

How serious a threat? Twenty-four of the accused were convicted of treason and sentenced to death or long prison terms in a December trial that local authorities billed as the most serious espionage case since 1975. Foreign diplomats here say that despite strong undercurrents of discontent in the South, there was no evidence—other than the prosecutor's claims—that the infiltrators posed a serious threat to the regime.

It is impossible for a visitor to measure the extent of potential opposition to Hanoi's rule. It is equally impossible to miss the deep differences between Vietnam's Northern and Southern regions over everything from attitudes toward work and ideology to the way to pronounce the name of the graceful, flowing *ao dai,* the national dress for women.

Some of these divisions reflect centuries of traditional dislike and disdain. Others are products of Hanoi's reluctant recognition of the continuing need for old Saigon's mercantile instincts that were centered in the Catholic community that fled the North in the 1950s after the Communists took over there.

A crash effort to nationalize industry and collectivize agriculture in 1978 brought the South to an economic standstill and triggered the mass exodus of South Vietnamese refugees by boat and overland. A parallel series of setbacks in the North's state-directed economy brought all Vietnam to the brink of disaster.

Making a virtue out of necessity, Hanoi reversed course. Many former Saigon executives were permitted to continue managing their businesses, getting higher salaries than directors of state-run firms and even sharing in local-currency profits. Merchants were allowed to resume foreign trade without central-government direction.

The results of this relative freedom are startlingly apparent. South Vietnam's former capital, with a population of only 3.5 million, accounts for an estimated 40 percent of the economic output of the entire nation of 60 million people.

Two thirds of this is open-market production outside direct government controls. Alone, seafood and agricultural shipments by Ho Chi Minh City entrepreneurs provide more than one fifth of Vietnam's total export earnings, far more than Hanoi earns from all its overseas trade.

Peasant farmers in the South's rich Mekong River delta region grow half of the country's rice crop. Because their cooperation is essential for achieving national self-sufficiency in food, Hanoi has backed away from forcing them onto collective farms. That was tried in the late 1970s, but many peasants resisted by growing only enough rice for their own families, turning grain into easily hidden alcohol and slaughtering pigs for holiday celebrations instead of selling them to the state at controlled prices.

Zones plan unsuccessful. Another Northern failure in the South was the opening of "new economic zones" that were intended to develop unused land and resettle 1 million city dwellers, including Saigon's thousands of bar girls and beggars.

Authorities soon discovered that much of the new-zone land was too poor to cultivate and that urban drifters had no talent for farming. Some resettled people still work on coffee, sugar and rubber plantations, but diplomats estimate that 40 percent of them simply left the zones. A good many of those are numbered among Ho Chi Minh City's 200,000 unemployed, who exist mainly by living off relatives.

Despite setbacks, officials in Hanoi insist that South Vietnam eventually will be reshaped in the North's hardline Marxist image. Says People's Committee member Vu Hac Bong: "We are determined to control basic goods essential for people's lives. This is a question of peace and war for us."

In the stubborn South, this could be a long conflict—longer, even, than the three decades it took the North to achieve military victory.

'WHERE IS MY FATHER?'[3]

"Remember me because I'll come back for you. I love you—Al." Those words scrawled on the back of a yellowing snapshot are all that Nguyen Minh Tam knows of his American father. The photo of a young GI with his arm around Tam's mother helped him endure the special alienation reserved for a half-breed outcast born into poverty and bigotry in Vietnam. When Tam was 10 he missed a rendezvous with his fleeing mother and spent the next four years living in a one-room apartment in Ho Chi Minh City with his aunt and grandmother. He was expelled from school with no explanation. He went for years without a new toy or new clothes. When Tam arrived in Long Beach, Calif., last month—his features hauntingly like those of the lean, unsmiling American in the photo—he submitted to an awkward hug and asked his mother almost immediately: "Where is my father?"

Tam is one of the lucky ones. An estimated 8,000 to 15,000 children were sired by American servicemen and civilians during the Vietnam War, and the vast majority remain in Vietnam today, left behind like broken-down jeeps. In a society proud of its ethnic purity, they are ostracized for their black or Caucasian features, unwelcome reminders that Vietnamese women slept with the enemy. Abandoned by their fathers, some have been rejected by their mothers as well and left to scavenge in the streets, where they are called *bui doi*—dust of life. They are the living legacy of the U.S. presence in Vietnam, and 10 years after the war their fate remains

[3]Reprint of an article by Melinda Beck, staff writer. *Newsweek*. 105:54–57. Ap. 15, '85. Copyright © 1985 by *Newsweek*. Reprinted by permission.

mired in bureaucratic tangles and the fickle relations of two nations that treat their common offspring as little better than political pawns.

Vietnam has said it will let every Amerasian leave immediately—if the United States officially accepts responsibility for them. But Washington still resists bilateral negotiations with Hanoi. Instead, since 1982 the Reagan administration has been accepting some Amerasians through a United Nations refugee program designed for Vietnamese boat people. The State Department says the Orderly Departure Program is working. But in fact it is far from orderly, and at the current pace—one flight a month brings Amerasians from Ho Chi Minh City to Bangkok—it could take 10 years to bring them all to American shores.

Today, the half-American children are less visible on Vietnamese streets than in the years just after the war. Many have scattered to outlying provinces and some Vietnamese mothers blacken their hair with shoe polish to disguise their appearance. Hanoi denies any official policy of discrimination, but many Amerasians tell of being teased and beaten by their pure Vietnamese peers. Mostly, they have grown up as hardened survivors among the poorest of Vietnam's poor. While few of their mothers were actually prostitutes, most were working-class girls. Tran Ngot Guy, 16, dropped out of school to support his family selling cigarettes. He does not know his father's name or his whereabouts, only that his mother worked for the U.S. Army near Da Nang. "How far is America?" he asks a Western visitor.

Those who wish to leave must hazard a perilous course through the Vietnamese bureaucracy. Phuong, a 14-year-old orphan who didn't know his last name, walked from Da Nang to Ho Chi Minh City last year when he heard about the refugee program, and he was allowed to leave within months. But most must apply first at local security offices, then at provincial offices and finally in Ho Chi Minh City—a Kafkaesque process that can take years and require as many as 30 signatures and multiple fees. (Between unofficial charges and outright bribes, the average escape is two to three taels of gold—about $1,000.) "These people live from day to day not knowing what their status is," says one ODP official. "Some of the forms they fill out make tax forms look easy."

Dealing with American authorities can be almost as frustrating. Since no U.S. officials can work in Ho Chi Minh City, United Nations staffers interview those who win exit visas and pass the information on to U.S. personnel in Bangkok for approval. Often, the U.S. and Vietnamese files don't match. And given Vietnam's lack of computerized records, if the U.S. side wants information on a particular child, "someone is liable to have to look through thousands of pieces of paper to find it," says one resettlement worker. Still, most Amerasians are approved quickly; if birth certificates are missing, U.S. staffers can now accept old letters, photos or even the child's physical appearances as proof of his American ties. But mothers and other relatives who wish to emigrate must prove they are related, and often they lack proper papers. The traditional Vietnamese family register, the Ho Kau, is one form of proof—but many Amerasians were never registered, lest they taint the family name.

The scrutiny is necessary, U.S. officials say, because as word of the departure program spreads, so do abuses. Stories abound of some wealthy Vietnamese "buying" Amerasians from desperate mothers and forging documents to send themselves or their children out with them. Yet while some such "piggy-backing" families make it to the United States, some real family members must stay behind. Fourteen-year-old Le Thi Thien and her grandmother spent two years filling out application forms so that the family could emigrate; Thien's grandmother sold her house to pay exit fees. In the end, only Thien was allowed to come through ODP. "At first I didn't want to go," she said through an interpreter when she arrived in Minneapolis last month. "But my grandmother talked me into it. She told me I would have a better chance here."

Those Amerasians who successfully navigate the bureaucratic shoals soon find themselves in an emotional and cultural limbo. The majority do emigrate with relatives and are sent to refugee-processing centers in Indochina for orientation into American ways. In Bataan, the largest of the camps, the training is in practical basics: how to flush a toilet, use a post office, buy food in a supermarket and read help-wanted ads. The émigrés learn rudimentary English and experience Western living in a full-scale model home, complete with a vacuum cleaner, a blender and a video-cassette recorder playing "Superman" tapes. They are also offered job training. "Don't think you deserve to go on welfare," one American teacher tells students.

Once in the United States, however, many families do end up on welfare—at least temporarily. And because sponsoring community groups are scarce, some are crowded into tiny apartments in big cities. One mother who trekked 250 miles to bring her Amerasian son to America was settled in a New York welfare apartment and now fears for him in a crime-ridden Bronx high school. Another, Nguyen Thi Sen, shares a crowded flat in Rochester, N.Y., with two more refugee mothers and their three Amerasian children. "Who will want me? I am old and have a language problem," she says.

Those Amerasians who emigrate alone—"unaccompanied minors"—come directly to the United States and are placed with foster families under the auspices of Catholic and Lutheran agencies. The transition from a hardened street life to a suburban middle-class home can be wrenching. Many arrive in poor health, suffering everything from parasites to malnourishment; almost all need dental care. Their emotional scars take even longer to heal. Some barely understand why they have been sent to America and sense only rejection again. Taken to lunch shortly after he arrived in Jackson, Miss., 15-year-old Dat Quoc Le (not his real name) would say only, "Eat. Very sad. Think my mama."

Volunteer workers say some Amerasians invent elaborate fantasies when they first arrive—possibly to cover old wounds. "Dat" told his foster family he had escaped from Vietnam by boat across the shark-infested South China Sea and spent eight months in a refugee camp eating nothing but "rice-chicken soup, rice-chicken soup, bleah!" (Case workers know for a fact he left Vietnam on a 747, spent 10 days in Bangkok and flew on to the United States.) One 14-year-old first said that her Vietnamese adoptive family had hired her out as a servant. Later, she said her grandfather sent her out to work. Noting that her vocabulary is that of a street urchin, volunteers still don't think they've heard the whole story. "I think we're going to hear that her grandfather threw her out of the house and she lived as a street child for two years," says Lou

Johnson, director of the refugee-minors program for Mississippi Catholic Charities.

Typically, the Amerasians go through pendular mood swings as they adjust to American life—ranging from fear to frustration to guilt about family left behind. Many suffer from chronic low self-esteem. "They have attitudes like, 'Anybody in the past who's ever meant anything to me has abandoned me, so I'm not going to let you get close to me because you're going to do the same thing'," says psychologist Dennis Hunt, director of the refugee-minors program in northern Virginia. Those with black fathers face special problems—and some exhibit surprisingly strong hatred of their racial heritage. Unsuspecting volunteers placed one Afro-Amerasian girl with a black foster family in Jackson—and her reaction toward her well-meaning foster father was pure rage. Later she said she had promised her mother never to let a black man touch her like her father had touched her mother.

The pressure to succeed is enormous—in part because Amerasians often see America as their last chance for acceptance. Many threaten or attempt suicide at some point. For all the adjustment problems, however, there are rewards. Adapting quickly to life in East Bethel, Minn., Le Thi Thien asked her foster family to call her "Linda," the name she says her father gave her, and pronounced America "amazing." And, says Hunt, "there's the kid who arrives at the airport and tears come to his eyes—because he's never seen so many people who look like him."

In all, 2,408 Amerasians have emigrated through the Orderly Departure Program, and controversy continues over the thousands remaining in Vietnam. U.S. officials say they would accept more if Vietnam would send them. Vietnam contends that America still requires too much proof of their U.S. parentage. In 1982 Congress passed a law that should have eased the situation: it granted all Amerasians born in Southeast Asia since 1950 first visa preference under U.S. immigration law and loosened requirements for proving their American ties. But the State Department has refused to use the bill on the ground that it contained no provisions for family members. "They have thrown every brick possible in the roadway on this matter," fumes Rep. Stewart McKinney

of Connecticut, the bill's leading sponsor, who has called for
House oversight hearings into the issue. Other critics are just as
frustrated. "Where there's a will, there's a way, and we have no
will," fumes John Shade, former director of the Pearl Buck Foun-
dation. "The U.S. government has never accepted the fact that
these are the progeny of our own loins."

About 150 Amerasians with welcoming American fathers
have emigrated through another route: as U.S. citizens. Human
Rights Advocates International, a public-interest law firm, contends that all the Amerasians should be recognized as citizens and
expedited on that basis. But U.S. officials say that to qualify for
citizenship, a child born overseas must have an identifiable American parent who is willing to legitimate him. (In 22 states a father
can do so without marrying the mother.) "We don't have fathers
with names, let alone fathers who would legitimate the birth,"
says the State Department's Frank Sieverts. Still, HRAI attorneys
say that even where some desperate fathers have taken legitima-
tion steps, they can't seem to satisfy the U.S. and Vietnamese
bureaucracies. "Two sovereign nations are playing games at the
expense of children," charges HRAI's Charles Printz.

Where possible, government staffers make some efforts to contact fathers and determine whether they want to see their offspring. "The vast majority say, 'No way. I have a different life
now'," says one U.S. official formerly with the program. Some fathers are willing to provide assistance—but only if their Amerasian children do not intrude on their present lives. One former
Special Forces officer, now a high-ranking intelligence official in
Washington, made such a request when he learned that his Amerasian daughter and her mother were emigrating. Describing
himself as a "standard male shit," he told *Newsweek*'s Nicholas
M. Horrock he had last seen the girl when she was six months
old. He left her mother with a house, a bank account and a sewing
machine, and later married another Vietnamese. "I have a family
now," he said. "I can't let anything intrude on our happiness."

It is not uncommon for such notations to be put into veterans'
service records. Their emigrating Amerasian children and their
mothers are generally never told. So most children go on dreaming
of joyous reunions, clinging to crumpled letters and scanning every

face they see for a resemblance to an old photo. Most will never
shake the mixture of hope and hurt and wonder, though some har-
bor the sad belief that they must travel much further in life to be
worthy of a father's love. Ten-year-old Tuan, now living with his
mother in Rochester, hopes to become an aircraft mechanic like
his father. That way he can "earn a lot of money and find him
when he grows older," Tuan says. "Then I will be able to take
care of him and he will want me."

A BITTER PEACE: LIFE IN VIETNAM[4]

. . . We flew to Ho Chi Minh City—Saigon—on a Soviet-
built Antonov turboprop plane. If Hanoi had been untouched for
30 or 40 years, Ho Chi Minh City looked precisely the way it had
in 1973, when I was last there, except that the streets were far less
congested. The Majestic Hotel on the riverfront had the same fly-
specked 1950's-vintage Pan American World Airways pictures on
its walls, though the hotel was now called the Cuu Long and was
state owned.

Many of the restaurants I had remembered from the past were
still functioning. Givral's, the French patisserie, was still baking
croissants. The bars that had lined the downtown streets when the
Americans were there had been shut or converted into antique
shops.

On Dong Khoi (General Uprising) Street (Tu Do to the
Americans, Rue Catinat to the French), beggar urchins were selling peanuts and yelling, "Hey, you!" just as they used to when the
Americans were there. But now these were not Vietnamese beggars. I saw with stunned sorrow that many of them had strikingly
American faces—the young Amerasians whose situation in the
country is so desperate.

[4]Excerpted from an article by Craig R. Whitney, an assistant managing editor of *The New York Times*.
New York Times Magazine. 133:59–63. O. 30, '83. Copyright © 1983 by the *New York Times Magazine*.
Reprinted by permission.

I was surprised in Ho Chi Minh City, as I had been in Hanoi, by what the authorities allowed to go on under their noses. The first few times I left the hotel alone and tried to make my way up the street, I was attacked by money changers offering 170, 180 dong to the dollar, about 20 times the official rate, and the Amerasian children followed me all the way to the cathedral, asking for handouts. Other days, the sidewalk was completely clear, the street people eyeing me nervously from across the road, apparently after a police sweep; a few hours later, the parasites and black marketeers were back at their usual positions.

Only once was I made aware of being followed by a plainclothes policeman. He gave a dirty look to a small Amerasian boy who had been pestering me to buy him a shirt; the kid then whispered to me, "C.I.D.," the American G.I.'s code for Military Police narcotics detectives. I felt, and was warned, that the only possible purpose he could have in following me was to report on any Vietnamese I spoke with.

I tried to challenge this prohibition twice. The first man I visited, a person with relatives in the United States who had applied for permission to leave Vietnam to join them, welcomed me to his house in a rainstorm, but nervously looked out the door and after 10 minutes asked me to please leave before the police came. Apparently he feared a search and interrogation about my presence. I went next door to a restaurant, and two plainclothes agents were pointed out to me. When I left, at the nervous urging of the restaurant owner, they did not follow me and I assumed my host was getting the questioning he feared. He wrote later to his family through the censored mail that he was grateful for my visit.

The second time, visiting a widow whose husband had been the night watchman in The Times's office, my presence caused such a sensation among the hordes of excited children in the neighborhood that I left her after only a few minutes, hoping to avoid the arrival of the police. She, too, hoped somehow to emigrate to the United States.

Ho Chi Minh City, I felt at moments like this, was still an occupied city, occupied by the Communist Northerners who run the country and still don't trust the Southern Vietnamese for collaborating with us. But, according to Nguyen Co Thach, the Foreign Minister, "there was no bloodbath. We had 1.5 million people in re-education camps, and 10,000 of them are still there now. But not one of them was killed in capital punishment. That's no good." Perhaps he and Pham Van Dong and Vo Nguyen Giap, the North Vietnamese commander who won the war, and the others had seen enough blood and death to reject the idea of a purge.

Stalin would have known how to re-educate these people, and no one would ever have come back. He would have known how to stop the black market and how to get the jobless off the streets of Ho Chi Minh City, too. Pol Pot, in Cambodia, and not Ho Chi Minh's successors in Vietnam, had turned out to be the last true Stalinist in Asia, contrary to all American expectations during the war.

True, the bloodbath never came. But another kind of death— of any hope of a decent life here under the new regime—does drive many of the Vietnamese to try to leave.

When or whether those who apply will get exit visas is hard to tell. Through the Orderly Departure Program, set up under the United Nations High Commissioner for Refugees in 1979, Vietnamese who can get permission from their Government to leave, and from some other country to let them in, are allowed to leave.

Mr. Tuyen told me that so far the Vietnamese had granted 18,000 exit visas to people wanting to go to the United States under the program, but up to the time I talked to him in September, only 12,200, according to American officials, had been given permission to enter the country. Mr. Tuyen acknowledged that his office had received 32,500 applications from Ho Chi Minh City alone—equal to the total number of people who have been allowed out under the program since it began.

There has been a gradual and steady decline in illegal departures, which have totaled about one million since 1975, apparently because refugees have been refused entry in many places. For example, "boat people" arriving in Hong Kong now must choose between moving on to another port or spending the rest of their lives in a closed refugee camp.

The Communists explain that these people want to leave because they grew accustomed to artificially high living standards during the American occupation. But I suspect the real reason is that in Vietnam they simply have no future.

Take the case of a young man who had been studying medicine in Saigon when he was drafted into the South Vietnamese Army in the early 1970's. After the defeat, he was no longer eligible to continue his medical studies, because he had been drafted into the wrong army. His mother was killed in the war with the French in 1951; his father was killed in fighting with the United States Marines in 1967; but for being in the wrong place at the wrong time, he was now consigned to a life as a tour-bus driver at 130 dong a month.

Ly Cong Chanh, a former official of the Provisional Revolutionary Government who is now vice chairman of the Ho Chi Minh City People's committee, told me that there were still more than 200,000 people without jobs. I met one foreign resident of the city who thought the real figure was much higher, as much as 60 percent of the work force.

Mr. Chanh sounded resigned. "More than 700,000 people left the city for new economic zones, or for their native villages, after liberation," he said, "but about 10,000 of them couldn't survive in the zones and came back. We tell them that if they stay here, they'll get no house and no job, but we don't move them out to the countryside by force. If we did, they'd just come back again. It's no use," he said.

I asked to see one of the new economic zones and was taken to a sugarcane farm called Nhi Xuan not far from Ho Chi Minh City in what used to be an artillery free-fire zone during the war. It was obviously meant to be a showcase; the guest book showed a parade of foreign dignitaries, including a number of predictably enthusiastic Russians.

Still, it was very poor: a line of tin-roofed wooden shacks along an irrigation canal, packed earth floors, no electricity or potable water except rainwater from earthenware cisterns. The people grew their own food, and collected rations—a pound of meat and a pound of fish per month, per family; some people raised chickens or geese.

This was a model zone built by "youth volunteers," who dug the canals, turned the sod and built the houses for the refugees who came later. I gathered from various conversations that many of these volunteers were renegades or former soldiers or drug addicts given a chance to atone for their misdeeds and find a better life after two or three years of hard work. The families who came to live and work on the farm, I was told, got their houses free and an allowance of 20,000 dong to get started.

Mr. Chanh, talking to me late in the ornate 19th-century city hall in Ho Chi Minh City, told me the authorities hoped gradually to solve the problem of unemployment there by putting people to work on the few nearby industrial development projects—a rubber plantation, a hydroelectric dam, the oil exploration project being worked on with Russian help at the former beach resort of Vung Tau. But for the most part, the economy of Ho Chi Minh City is still based on small-scale trading and commerce, a service economy built up during the boom years when 500,000 G.I.'s were there—200,000 households in Saigon still earn their living this way today, according to official Vietnamese statistics.

"We're trying to reduce them little by little and transform them from trading to production," Mr. Chanh said. "We have to do this step by step."

Fits and starts might be a more accurate description of Vietnamese economic policy since 1975. At first, pledging a gradual transition to socialism, the new Communist rulers left the farmers and merchants of the South alone. Then, in March 1978, the bigger trading firms, many owned by Chinese businessmen from Cholon, were closed and nationalized.

The course was partly reversed again in late 1979 to avert a complete economic collapse. The latest measures, instituted last May, penalize small businesses with heavy taxes.

"We have had a lot of experience in war," Mr. Chanh said, "but not in administering the affairs of a big city like this. We have made many mistakes. I am 59, and Mai Chi Tho, the chairman of the city committee, is 60. We have to train our successors, so they won't make the mistakes we made."

The mistakes have alienated many South Vietnamese who welcomed the Communist victory in 1975. A few, like Ngo Ba Thanh, a professor educated in Paris and New York who spent years in jail during the rule of President Nguyen Van Thieu, try to bridge the gaps in understanding.

"Most of the mistakes that have been made are the result of trying to move too fast," she said, speaking in a rush of fluent English. "And there are great differences between the North and the South. I tell the people in the party that the revolution would not have been won with the party alone. The people played a great role and must be allowed to continue to play a great role. The party authorities sometimes claim that they can do anything they want, even if it violates the laws on the books, because in our system the party plays the leading role. But it's more complicated than that."

"Pham Van Dong told me that I had to be very patient," she said. "He pointed out to me this Cabinet minister who was a rice farmer 40 years ago, and that one who had been illiterate, and said I should give these people a chance, should be tolerant of their mistakes."

She also said she did not agree with many of her friends in the South who complained about not having a big enough role in the Government. "We in the South have lots of experience in overthrowing governments," she said with a laugh, "not in making them run better."

Other people in the South Vietnamese educated class aren't as optimistic as Mrs. Thanh, or as well treated, and many who hated the Thieu regime now say they were wrong to think that nothing could be worse than the corruption and repression of that period.

"The Thieu Government collapsed because its leaders were unworthy of the name," a former student told me. "But now many people who were glad to see it go feel that the new Government isn't so gay, either. They've lost their illusions. They don't like having to apply to the ward committee and pay a bribe even to get permission to go visit their relatives in the Mekong Delta for a week. But they still delude themselves. A lot of them talk about how the Americans are going to land with helicopters and sweep the Communists away. The Americans—imagine!"

I asked if people blamed the United States for the defeat—as some Americans blame themselves for not providing Thieu with enough military aid to fight off the Communist advances. "I don't blame the Americans at all," he said. "They gave plenty of money and help, and it wasn't their fault that our generals and leaders couldn't put it to proper use. It is our country. It was ours to defend—we should have defended it ourselves."

That is precisely why the Communists won, I said—they really believed it. He shrugged. "It's true," he said.

Ho Chi Minh's saying, "There is nothing more precious than independence and freedom," now stands above nearly every door in Vietnam. Many people in the South put it there in the last days of April 1975, hoping to show the Communists their hearts were in the right place. Even with all the help they have from the Russians, I concluded, the Vietnamese have independence, but freedom, no, not now.

Many of the Communist war veterans I had met in my two-week trip had emotionally expressed their wishes for peace, for their children, my children, all our children together. We were veterans of the same war, and we felt, strange as it may seem, a sense of shared responsibility for what we had done to each other. Perhaps, eventually, passions will cool and we will, like the French before us, extend the hand of aid and conciliation to this fiercely independent, xenophobic people.

The only flight out of Saigon to the West is an Air France jumbo jet that arrives practically empty from Paris via Bangkok every Thursday and goes back full of refugees. For the first time in my experience in Communist countries, my Vietnamese hosts let me take pictures in the airport as I interviewed those who were leaving. Finally, when the shuttle bus pulled out, their relatives shrieked their names desperately from the observation platform.

There was nervous tension among these people as we went through yet another ticket check on the gangway; they would not believe they were really leaving until the plane started rolling down the runway. But as the doors were sealed and the engines began turning, I looked back into the cabin and saw that it would be impossible to continue interviewing them. Their native land was rushing past the windows, and tears were streaming down their faces, and so there was no need to ask any more questions.

II. CONTINUING CONFLICT:
VIETNAM'S OCCUPATION OF CAMBODIA

EDITOR'S INTRODUCTION

Vietnam's invasion and occupation of Cambodia in 1978 has been a source of world-wide concern. Cambodia's neighbor Thailand now stands in a particularly threatened position and has joined with other nations in the Pacific in an organization called ASEAN, which opposes the occupation and hopes to negotiate a solution. The occupation of Cambodia has alienated world opinion and cost Vietnam dearly in economic assistance from Western nations, which it badly needs if it is to become a modern, industrialized nation. The United States has placed an embargo on trade and economic help to Vietnam until the Cambodian issue is resolved. Yet Vietnam shows no signs of curtailing its expansionist policy, and not only continues to maintain an army of 200,000 troops in Cambodia but has also stepped up its attack on guerrilla resistance groups. Cambodia has become "Vietnam's Vietnam."

In the first article in this section, Martin F. Herz reviews the overthrow by the Vietnamese of the Khmer Rouge, the Communist regime in Cambodia headed by Pol Pot and supported by China, and their installation of a puppet government led by Heng Samrin. He then addresses the problem of the guerrilla resistance in Cambodia today and faults the United States for its failure to send military assistance to the group led by Son Sann, an independent nationalist with no ties to the Communists. A second article, by Jacques Bekaert, reprinted from *The Nation,* examines the guerrilla factions in more detail—the group headed by Prince Sihanouk, the independent nationalists led by Son Sann, and the Khmer Rouge—and the formation of their awkward alliance against the Vietnamese. In two following articles, reprinted from *The Department of State Bulletin,* the official position of the American government is expressed. In the first, Paul D. Wolfowitz, Assistant Secretary of State for East Asian and Pacific Affairs, discusses the plight of Cambodia, first under the Khmer Rouge, which killed at least a million of the population in an effort to eradicate every trace of the traditional Cambodian culture, and then under the Vietnamese, who have settled the country with 500,000 of their own people, making Cambodia a subject colony. Finally, an address by Jeane Kirkpatrick, former U. S. Representative to the United Nations, deals with international efforts to bring pressure on Vietnam. Despite these efforts, she observes, Vietnam persists in its colonialization of its neighbor and has recently stepped up its efforts to eradicate guerrilla resistance.

THE SCANDAL OF CAMBODIA[1]

The occupation of Cambodia (Kampuchea) by the Vietnamese, who invaded it in 1978 and installed a puppet government that remains in power today, is fully comparable to the Soviet invasion of Afghanistan. Why then has it received so much less public attention?

One reason is that in spite of its imperialist and colonialist aspects, the Vietnamese conquest relieved Cambodia of an even more oppressive Communist regime, that of the Khmer Rouge (at one time headed by Pol Pot) which, in the period from 1975 to 1978, probably managed to kill between one and two million of Cambodia's population. Compared with the genocidal psychopaths of the Khmer Rouge, the Vietnamese-imposed regime looks not so bad. By any other standard, however, the situation in Cambodia is a tragedy of immense proportions.

The terms "imperialist" and "colonialist" are strictly applicable to the occupation. Vietnam has a history of eating Cambodia, chunk by chunk. Most of what used to be known as South Vietnam was at one time Cambodian territory—not just Cambodian-administered but territory inhabited by Cambodians. The Vietnamese-imposed regime of Heng Samrin, even if it is less terrible

[1]Reprint of an article by Martin F. Herz, author and Oscar Iden Research Professor at Georgetown University. *Commentary*. 73:52–53. F. '83. Copyright © 1982 by *Commentary*. Reprinted by permission.

than that of its predecessor, is therefore abhorred by the Cambodians who have hated and feared the Vietnamese for centuries. That hatred and fear, as a matter of fact, were at the root of the deposition in 1970 of Prince Norodom Sihanouk, whose collusion with the Vietnamese Communists had become a public scandal.

There are four contenders for power in Cambodia at present: (1) the Vietnamese, who keep Heng Samrin in power with 200, 000 occupation troops and who have the full support of the Soviet Union in their rape of Cambodia; (2) the remnants of the genocidal Khmer Rouge, who are on the Thai-Cambodian border and enjoy the support of the Chinese People's Republic; (3) the discredited Prince Sihanouk, at one time widely regarded as a true neutralist but who finished himself in Cambodia when he consented to be used by the Khmer Rouge in their drive for power in 1970—even though later he became their prisoner and still later denounced his former allies and jailors; (4) the anti-Communist Khmer National Liberation Front of Son Sann, also located on the Thai-Cambodian border, with troops in the field that are still small in comparison with those of the Khmer Rouge, but with a vast reservoir of good will and support in Cambodia.

It is said, correctly, that if the Cambodians were given the choice between a return of the Khmer Rouge and a continuation of the present foreign-imposed Heng Samrin regime, they would very likely choose the latter. But why should they be forced to make such a hideous choice?

Many observers believe that if Son Sann were given support in arms and money, he would draw to himself all those who want to rid his country of the Vietnamese. It is probable that even some of the Khmer Rouge troops would come over to him.

This being so, one would think that the West—not only the United States but all countries concerned for freedom and self-determination in Southeast Asia—would help Son Sann. Yet no such help (except in the "humanitarian" domain, which unfortunately does not translate into political or military power of influence) is being provided. Indeed, every time the question of the Cambodian delegation comes up in the United Nations, the U.S. —together with the West Europeans, the non-Communist Southeast Asians in ASEAN, and a majority of the remaining countries—hold their noses and vote for the Khmer Rouge ("Democratic Kampuchea") in order not to legitimate the Vietnamese aggression and occupation.

All this stands in scandalous contrast to the sympathy and support being given to Son Sann's counterparts in Afghanistan. Of course, there is one very important difference between Cambodia and Afghanistan. In the latter country, where the objective is to force the Russians out, Chinese and Western interests appear to coincide. In the case of Cambodia, however, the Chinese, in opposing the Soviet-backed Vietnamese, are stuck (or seem to think they are stuck) with the Khmer Rouge.

In Afghanistan, Chinese opposition to Soviet imperialism has not led to support for a Communist faction. It is possible that in time and with appropriate encouragement the Chinese could be brought to a similar position in Cambodia. Such encouragement would have to include Western support for the forces of Son Sann. Ironically the Chinese themselves are beginning to help Son Sann a little—but they are careful to give him considerably less than they give the Khmer Rouge.

The tragedy of the Cambodian liberation movement is that at the very time when it has an excellent chance of lighting a fire under the Vietnamese colonial occupation, Son Sann is being weakened through an association with the Khmer Rouge forced on him by the ASEAN countries and the U.S.

Thus in late November 1981, at the suggestion in Singapore and with the support of Thailand, a "loose coalition government" for Cambodia was worked out in Bangkok which would have a President (presumably Sihanouk), a Prime Minister (presumably Son Sann), a Vice Premier (Khmer Rouge), but in which, according to the press statements, "each faction would retain its identity and be free to propagate its own distinctive political program and philosophy for the future of Cambodia." Son Sann, in order not to be accused of ruining any chances for ASEAN support, agreed in principle. Sihanouk's representative said the Prince would go along with anything the others could agreed on. The Khmer Rouge said they would give their response later.

The agreement is of course unworkable—but if it goes into effect, it would be a hunting license for the various contenders to secure the foreign aid they need in order to drive the Vietnamese out of their country, after which the agreement contemplates "free elections conducted by the United Nations."

Everything now depends on whether the non-Communist resistance led by Son Sann can get the kind of assistance that will enable it to compete on at least even terms with the China-backed Khmer Rouge. (Prince Sihanouk, while he confuses the political equation, is not a major factor now.) Singapore and Malaysia have made oblique and elliptical statements perhaps indicating that if the coalition government really came to pass, and if Son Sann were a "prime minister" rather than just the leader of a liberation movement, they would find ways of helping the nationalists—or of transmitting help to them.

In this situation the position of the United States may become crucial. Public statements so far indicate that the U.S. will continue to provide "humanitarian" aid to Son Sann. But humanitarian aid alone will not enable him to compete with the murderous Khmer Rouge; and unless Son Sann can show that the agreement has opened the way to concrete aid for the anti-Communist cause, he risks being accused by his supporters of having been outmaneuvered by the Communists. As he once put it in a characteristically Cambodian metaphor: "I am a buffalo and the Khmer Rouge are a tiger. You want to put us under the yoke to pull the Cambodian cart out of the mud together. All right, I will go under the yoke with them—but then you will have to make me into a tiger. Otherwise what will happen to me is what happens when a buffalo tries to cooperate with a tiger."

The issue is not whether American forces are to be committed; that question is a red herring. The issue is whether, after all the misfortunes that Cambodia has suffered—including its abandonment by the United States in 1975—we have a right to turn our backs on people who are struggling for freedom and who only ask to be given as much support from the West as the Chinese are giving their own protégés.

Nobody can tell how the situation will come out if we help the forces fighting for the liberation of Cambodia. But it can be predicted with mathematical certainty that if no such aid is given, if the Khmer Rouge remain the principal resistance, Cambodia will be slowly and methodically digested by Vietnam and will eventually disappear as an independent country. Having abandoned Cambodia once in 1975, the United States would have abandoned it yet another time, when only a small effort might have given that country at least a fighting chance to regain its independence.

ON THE LONG ROAD TOWARD PHNOM PENH[2]

When the shell exploded, a couple of hundred yards from us, the soldiers I was with did not bother to stop or take cover or even look around. For them, the whistle and blast of Vietnamese shells is—like the heavy rain, the sticky mud, the evergreen jungle—all part of the routine.

For the 1,500 soldiers of the MOULINAKA—the Movement of National Liberation of Kampuchea—life is more tedious than exciting. They live with hunger and sickness daily. Only rarely do they come in contact with Vietnamese troops, only rarely is the fighting fierce. If a battle is bloody enough it will warrant a few lines in the Bangkok papers, but for the most part these men are among the forgotten soldiers of a war that no one likes and few pay attention to.

The MOULINAKA is one of the three factions that make up the National Sihanoukist Army, a force of perhaps 5,000 men loyal to former Kampuchean leader Prince Norodom Sihanouk. Together with the 9,000 soldiers of the Khmer People's National Liberation Front under former Sihanouk adviser Son Sann and the 25,000 men of the Khmer Rouge, the Communist force led by former dictator Pol Pot, they form the armed opposition to the Vietnamese puppet regime that now rules Kampuchea. And since

[2]Reprint of an article by Jacques Bekaert, correspondent in the Far East for *The Nation*. *The Nation*. 236:41–44. Ja. 15, '83. Copyright © 1983 by *The Nation*. Reprinted by permission.

last June, when these three disparate and often disputatious groups agreed to set up a coalition government-in-exile, these troops have been fighting a stepped-up campaign against the Vietnamese soldiers who occupy their homeland.

"This is our hospital," says Col. Nhem Sophon, the MOULINAKA commander, pointing to a small building. It does indeed have a red cross on its side and a few primitive beds, but there is no medicine other than a few containers of aspirin. "More than half our people are sick," he adds sorrowfully. Tropical diseases are rife, malaria the most common.

Most of the guns in the MOULINAKA camp, in a clearing near the border with Thailand where the resistance forces are strongest, are Chinese. Last March the Sihanouk soldiers received a shipment from China of enough weapons for 3,000 men, including the AK-47 rifles that seem to be ubiquitous in this area.

"It is very reliable," Chak Sarik tells me, tapping his rifle. Once Prince Sihanouk's chief of protocol, Sarik is now the MOULINAKA's political spokesman and a budding marksman. When the Khmer Rouge took over Kampuchea in April 1975, Sarik fled the country and settled in the United States. Two years ago he returned to Kampuchea and joined the Sihanouk forces along the western border. Once prosperous, today he could probably fit his possessions in a knapsack. There are many like him in this region, intellectuals and politicians and businessmen learning the hard way the basic facts of guerrilla warfare.

The strange coalition that Sarik is fighting for is united perhaps in nothing but its desire to drive the Vietnamese out of Kampuchea. In that, it expressed the feelings of a majority of Kampucheans.

It was in December 1978 that Vietnam decided to invade Kampuchea and remove the brutal Khmer Rouge government of Pol Pot. Relations between the two countries had long been tense, and Pol Pot's sympathy for China made Kampuchea a potentially dangerous ally for Peking's territorial ambitions. The fact that many Kampucheans were suffering under the Khmer Rouge regime and world opinion was beginning to turn against it as its cruelties became known gave Hanoi confidence that an invasion would be welcomed both from within and without.

Three months later Pol Pot was indeed deposed, his army badly battered and reduced to occupying a few enclaves along the Thai border. And the Vietnamese troops were indeed first greeted as liberators by the Kampuchean populace. But, because of pressure from China and the five countries of the ASEAN alliance (Thailand, Malaysia, Singapore, Indonesia and the Philippines), the new Vietnamese puppet regime gained diplomatic recognition from almost no one (among non-Communist nations, only India) and was not allowed to claim the Kampuchean seat in the United Nations.

In the three years since, opposition to the puppet regime has been sporadic but it has grown, culminating in the formation of the tripartite coalition last June.

Of the coalition partners, the best organized is the National Liberation Front. It was begun in 1976 as the Association of Overseas Kampucheans by a small group of intellectuals living in France opposed to the Khmer Rouge government. It picked as its leader Son Sann, a man who had been one of Sihanouk's closest collaborators, a former Prime Minister, and founder and governor of the National Bank of Cambodia. Sann had publicly dissociated himself from both the Pol Pot regime and the republican government of Lon Nol, which was established after Sihanouk's overthrow in 1970, but he had not rallied to the Sihanouk government-in-exile and was seen as an independent nationalist.

Son Sann and his allies decided to launch a guerrilla war against the Khmer Rouge along the Thai border, and they secured the services of a former Lon Nol general, Dien Del, to lead it. But it was not until the Vietnamese invasion that their project gained a secure foothold: Thailand, worried about its proximity to the large Vietnamese Army in Kampuchea (reportedly 200,000 men), gave Son Sann's forces easy access to the border. Just across the border into Kampuchea, in a small village called Phum Sokh Sann (Village of Peace), the National Liberation Front was formally begun on October 9, 1979.

At the time the N.L.F. had fewer than 2,000 armed men and another few thousand civilian supporters. Aid was slow in coming. China, always interested in opposition to the Vietnamese, supplied some weapons, but most of its support went to the Khmer Rouge. It was not until 1981 that the first substantial shipment of arms came from Peking, and this has been followed by other deliveries. Today the N.L.F. claims close to 9,000 men in arms and control of more than 140,000 civilians, a tribute not only to Chinese support but to the perseverance of Son Sann and his friends.

Prince Sihanouk's contribution to the coalition is based on the National Sihanoukist Army and a political party known as the FUNCIPEC (an acronym for the United Front for an Independent, Neutral, Peaceful and Cooperative Cambodia).

Sihanouk has been a long time coming around to an alliance with other exiles. For nearly two years after the Vietnamese invasion he tried to work out a peaceful settlement with Hanoi. He wrote three letters to his old comrade Pham Van Dong, the Vietnamese Premier, proposing to discuss the future of Kampuchea as friends. He argued that although most of his compatriots preferred the Vietnamese to the bloody Khmer Rouge—he himself had no love for the Khmer Rouge, which killed five of his children—they would eventually grow restless under foreign dominance; Vietnam should not overextend its stay, he said, or it would create the impression that it was planning to make Kampuchea a colony. "Pham Van Dong never answered my letters," Sihanouk told me in 1981. "The third one came back unopened."

Deeply disappointed, in 1980 the Prince turned to the United States, asking for enough money and weapons for an army of 100,000 men. "I had no desire to fight," he said. "I just wanted to show the Vietnamese it was in everybody's interest to be reasonable and talk. It was also very important to be able to show my people I could protect them against the Khmer Rouge as well as against the Vietnamese." Washington of course had no desire to get involved again in Indochina and declined to give Sihanouk any military aid. Secretary of State Cyrus Vance suggested that he should concentrate instead on finding economic aid for Kampuchean refugees.

Sihanouk set up a government-in-exile in Pyongyang, North Korea, and in March 1981 launched his new party. At the same time he asked Gen. In Tam, a Prime Minister in the Lon Nol regime, to organize an army. Tam set up one force known as Oddar Tus in September 1981 in the border area of O'Smach, then made alliances with two other guerrilla forces: the Kreang Mung, led by Toun Chhay, a former aeronautic engineer active in the resistance since 1975, and the MOULINAKA, founded in August 1979 by a captain in Sihanouk's navy, Kong Sileah, and now under the command of Nhem Sophon.

The third part of the coalition, the Khmer Rouge, is still led by the same people who formed the Phnom Penh government in 1976—Pol Pot, Ta Mok, Son Sen and Ke Pauk. In December 1981 they announced they were putting an end to the Communist Party which they had used as their political arm, but recent intelligence reports indicate that the party, by whatever name, is alive and well.

Until last year, the Khmer Rouge had resisted the idea of a coalition, preferring to rely on its allies in Peking. But in negotiations last spring, Son Sann gave up most of his original demands and agreed to let the Khmer Rouge have the important post of foreign minister, as well as the vice presidency, in a coalition government-in-exile. The Khmer Rouge leaders must also have realized that they were not gaining in popularity among Kampucheans— even if their crimes have been exaggerated by Vietnamese propaganda, hardly anyone wants to see them back in power—and by joining with the nationlist forces they would gain the appearance of respectability they had long sought.

For their part, although there is no feeling of warmth toward the Khmer Rouge, the two nationalist groups realized that through a coalition they would gain the stature they need in order to be formally recognized by other governments and to receive military and economic assistance openly. (The coalition agreement stipulates, however, that each of the three groups gets to keep for itself any aid that comes in specifically earmarked for one or another of them.) Sihanouk became president of the new government, making him at least technically a head of state—even without much of a territory—and enabling him more easily to use his considerable political connections, especially among Third

World leaders. Son Sann was willing to remain in the background as a kind of *éminence grise.*

"This coalition is not my dream," Sihanouk told me a few days after the official inauguration of the coalition in Kuala Lumpur, Malaysia, last June 22. "I have always favored an alliance between the nationalists, between Son Sann and myself. But nowhere could we find real support for such an idea. We have been forced into this coalition. It is for us to make the best of it."

Sihanouk knows that an alignment with the Khmer Rouge has its problems. "But our people are increasingly worried about the Vietnamese presence in our country," he said. "And by now we know the Khmer Rouge. They will always be isolated, with no real support among the people. For the time being, we have no choice but to include them." He did not need to add that with its 25,000 soldiers and its close ties to China, the Khmer Rouge represents the main guerrilla threat to the Vietnamese.

Sihanouk nonetheless still hopes that negotiations with the Vietnamese are possible. "I am always ready to talk to the Vietnamese," he said. "We need a political solution that gives everybody a chance to save face." He is even willing to give up his present position if that will help. "My position as president of the coalition government is a temporary thing," he told me. "What matters is the supreme interests of my people—their independence, peace and dignity."

Sihanouk and Son Sann both expected that news of the coalition would not be initially well received among exile Kampucheans, but in fact the reception all along the Thai border—and even among fiercely anti-Khmer Rouge refugees in Western countries—has been quite positive. When Sihanouk visited three resistance camps in Kampuchea and one refugee settlement in Thailand last July he was welcomed, and his old charismatic magic was still very effective. As he said later, "The people don't like the Khmer Rouge but they want to see the Vietnamese withdraw from their country."

That is likely to take some time, however, and the cost will be high. Now that the rainy season is over, the Vietnamese may launch a new offensive. A year ago, Vietnamese troops began a

successful operation, with attacks on several Khmer Rouge positions and the capture of one N.L.F. village near the border. But
then they unexpectedly withdrew, perhaps because their losses
were too high or perhaps because of malaria and other diseases.
"From a military point of view the Vietnamese could win," said
a senior European diplomat recently, speaking of a possible new
offensive. "But what matters is the political and diplomatic
situation"—and a strong coalition government headed by a popular and skillful man like Sihanouk makes victory on that front difficult indeed for the Vietnamese.

The Prince is hopeful, but he is not optimistic. As he says, the
road to Phnom Penh is a long and hazardous one, and an independent and neutral Kampuchea is still more a dream than a reality.

CAMBODIA: THE SEARCH FOR PEACE[3]

I appreciate the opportunity to be here with you as we recall
the ongoing tragedy in Cambodia. The presence of so many people
here testifies to the deep and abiding concern that Americans have
for the people of Cambodia. It is also testimony to the grievous
miscalculation made by Hanoi when it invaded Cambodia. The
world has not forgotten Cambodia's plight. The problem for the
international community today is how peace and independence
can be restored to Cambodia by ending the present Vietnamese
occupation without permitting a recurrence of the Khmer Rouge
period.

The Human Tragedy

Few nations in history have experienced the cumulative disas-
ters and destruction which have engulfed Cambodia during the
past two decades. Hanoi's use of Cambodian territory in its war

[3]Reprint of a statement before the Conference on the Cambodian Crisis (Sept. 11, 1984) by Paul D.
Wolfowitz, U. S. Assistant Secretary of State for East Asian and Pacific Affairs. *Department of State Bulletin.*
84:51-54. N. '84. Copyright © 1984 by the U. S. Department of State. Reprinted by permission.

against the south and the attack on the Khmer Republic by the communist Khmer Rouge, with Hanoi's support, destroyed Cambodia's economy and made refugees of millions of ordinary Khmer who sought safety in Phnom Penh and other cities. The war's end in 1975 unleashed an even greater tragedy, one that the world still cannot fully comprehend.

The whole world knows of the horrors that the Khmer people suffered under Khmer Rouge rule. In their effort to eradicate every vestige of the old Cambodia, the Khmer Rouge tried to destroy a culture which had endured for more than a millennium. Thousands who had served previous governments were brutally murdered and buried in mass graves. The entire population was sent to the countryside with whatever possessions they could carry. Hospitals and schools were abandoned, Buddhism—the enbodiment of the Khmer soul—was banned, and traditional culture was suppressed. Murder and starvation took the lives of at least a million Cambodians, but the total number who died during the $3\frac{1}{2}$ years of Khmer Rouge rule will never be known.

Vietnam bears a heavy responsibility for the Khmer Rouge, whom it sponsored and supported. It was the Vietnamese Army which nearly destroyed Cambodia's Army in 1970, opening the way for the Khmer Rouge seizure of much of the countryside. The Vietnamese army continued to occupy major portions of eastern Cambodia until after 1973. Hanoi supplied the Khmer Rouge with the arms and supplies to battle the Khmer Republic, including the Russian-built rockets which terrorized the civilians of Phnom Penh.

For a while after 1975, Vietnam continued to defend the new regime in Cambodia. The few refugees to escape Cambodia told of terror, murder, and starvation. Attempts to inform the world of the tragedy inside Cambodia or assist the Khmer people were met by silence from Phnom Penh and denunciations from Hanoi, which called the refugees' reports an American-inspired plot. Many writers and scholars in the West could not or would not believe the evidence about the Khmer Rouge, and one even criticized published reports as "wild exaggeration and wholesale falsehood" in testimony before a U.S. congressional hearing on human rights in Cambodia. Vietnam, joined by the U.S.S.R. and its supporters, tried to defend Cambodia when the United Nations at last inquired into conditions inside Cambodia.

Vietnam, of course, had its own reasons for assisting the Khmer Rouge. Hanoi ultimately sought to control the Cambodian communists as thoroughly as it controlled those in South Vietnam and Laos. In this, it failed.

Having failed to dominate and control the Khmer Rouge, Hanoi decided to depose them and replace them with a more pliable communist regime. On Christmas Day, 1978, Vietnam invaded Cambodia and rapidly drove the Khmer Rouge from Phnom Penh, installing Heng Samrin, a former lieutenant of Pol Pot, as the leader of a new regime. Instead of solving the Cambodian problem, Vietnam's occupation has simply thrust it into a new phase, more threatening to the security of its neighbors and hardly any less threatening to the Khmer people.

Vietnam's claim that it invaded Cambodia to liberate the Khmer people from Pol Pot and that it remains there only to prevent his return to power is a thinly disguised deception. Vietnam, which had defended Pol Pot against international criticism, deposed him only when it became apparent that the Khmer Rouge were unwilling to accept Vietnam's leadership. Vietnam today rules Cambodia through a puppet regime comprised of many former followers of Pol Pot, including Heng Samrin himself. Khmer Rouge who still follow Pol Pot are welcomed back by the Heng Samrin regime. It has publicly said they are free to resume their lives after a brief period of political indoctrination. Noncommunists, however, receive no such welcome in Vietnamese-controlled Cambodia.

Beyond the continued warfare, the Khmer people now face the possibility of an end to their homeland, except as a name on the map, and the extinction of an ancient culture. Thousands of Vietnamese citizens are now settling throughout Cambodia, abetted and encouraged by Hanoi. While the actual number of Vietnamese immigrants is unknowable, except perhaps to the Vietnamese authorities, it is likely that hundreds of thousands of Vietnamese nationals have settled in Cambodia in the past 4 years. Willibald Pahr, former Austrian Foreign Minister and Chairman of the International Conference on Kampuchea, recently stated in a press conference that Vietnamese immigrants number 500,000 at a minimum.

Heng Samrin regime documents, moreover, instruct officials to assist Vietnamese, both former residents and new immigrants, in any way possible and to consult with the Vietnamese advisers before taking any action affecting Vietnamese settlers. Vietnamese soldiers serving in Cambodia are encouraged to settle in the country and marry Khmer women. Those who do so are to receive Cambodian citizenship. Vietnamese immigrants are also given extraterritorial status—violations of Cambodian laws are to be dealt with by the Vietnamese authorities, not Cambodian. Some new refugees from Cambodia report that villagers are required to provide housing and food to new Vietnamese settlers.

When combined with Vietnamese-imposed changes to Cambodian administration and Khmer society, this officially sponsored Vietnamese immigration raises serious questions about Hanoi's long-term intentions toward Cambodia. It will be the ultimate tragedy if Cambodia, decimated by war and famine, should now be extinguished as an entity, submerged, and colonized by its much larger, more powerful neighbor.

International Security Concerns and the World's Response

Beyond the human tragedy in Cambodia, the situation there is also a crisis for the international community because of its implications for the security of all nations, particularly those of Southeast Asia. Vietnam's invasion and occupation of Cambodia violates the UN Charter, which Vietnam signed, and threatens the system of collective security, embodied in the UN Charter, designed to preserve the independence and territorial integrity of all nations. No one lamented the demise of the Khmer Rouge, a regime detested everywhere. But Hanoi did not invade Cambodia for the purpose of returning Cambodia to its people. Instead, Vietnam installed a puppet regime of its own choosing, one comprised of former followers of Pol Pot and Khmer communists who had lived in Vietnam for many years, a regime that depends on a Vietnamese Army of occupation for its survival.

It should come as no surprise that Vietnam's invasion and occupation of Cambodia drew its most coherent response from the neighboring countries most directly threatened, the members of the Association of South East Asian Nations (ASEAN). ASEAN has taken the leading role in the search for a solution to the Cambodian crisis that can restore stability to the region and end the suffering of the Khmer people. That kind of solution must end Hanoi's occupation and prevent the Khmer Rouge from returning to power.

ASEAN's Proposals

ASEAN seeks a political settlement that would restore an independent, neutral Cambodia under a government freely chosen by the Cambodian people and posing no threat to any of its neighbors. The UN-sponsored International Conference on Kampuchea met in July 1981 with 94 countries sending delegates or observers. Vietnam and its friends in the Soviet bloc refused to attend. Its final declaration contained four elements:

• An agreement on a cease-fire by all parties . . . and withdrawal of all foreign forces from Kampuchea in the shortest time possible under the supervision and verification of a UN peacekeeping force/observer group.
• Appropriate arrangements to ensure that armed Kampuchean factions will not be able to prevent or disrupt the holding of free elections or intimidate or coerce the population in the electoral process; such arrangements should also ensure that they respect the results of the free elections.
• Appropriate measures for the maintenance of law and order . . . before the establishment of a new government resulting from those elections.
• The holding of free elections under United Nations supervision . . . ; all Kampucheans will have the right to participate in the elections.

The final declaration also calls on all states to pledge their respect for Cambodia's independence, territorial integrity, and nonaligned status. These principles were endorsed in successive resolutions of the UN General Assembly.

In its various efforts to find a political solution, ASEAN has sought to work out the framework of a settlement which preserves

the legitimate security concerns of Cambodia's neighbors, including Vietnam. ASEAN has repeatedly offered Hanoi the opportunity to work out the arrangements for a settlement. Vietnam has
totally rejected the framework of the International Conference on
Kampuchea. ASEAN has implicitly agreed to work for a solution
through some other process as long as the key elements of Vietnamese withdrawal and elections are preserved. In 1983, Thai
Foreign Minister Siddhi offered to go to Hanoi for talks if Vietnam would pull its forces in Cambodia back 30 kilometers from
the Thai border. Vietnam refused. In September 1983, the
ASEAN foreign ministers issued a joint "Appeal for Kampuchean
Independence." In that appeal, they proposed a territorially
phased Vietnamese withdrawal, coupled with an international
peacekeeping force and reconstruction aid in the areas vacated, as
part of a Vietnamese commitment to a complete withdrawal and
elections. No mention was made of the International Conference
on Kampuchea. Hanoi rejected this proposal as well.

This year, ASEAN has again sought to find a settlement for-
mula which preserves Vietnam's legitimate security interests.
During Vietnamese Foreign Minister Thach's visit to Jakarta,
Indonesian President Soeharto signaled the possibility of move-
ment on important negotiating points. Thach rejected those pro-
posals also. The ASEAN foreign ministers have formally adopted
Prince Sihanouk's call for national reconciliation, including the
Heng Samrin faction. Vietnam remains silent.

Vietnam's conduct in Cambodia has isolated it internationally.
The majority of nonaligned nations have joined ASEAN, Western
Europe, Japan, and the United States in condemning Vietnam's
aggression. Most of our allies and friends have joined us in supporting ASEAN's strategy of political and economic pressure on
Vietnam to convince Hanoi that a political settlement in Cambodia is in its own interest. Australia suspended its economic assistance program in 1979. Japan and many European countries have
reduced or frozen their own programs. Japan has also offered financial support for implementation of ASEAN's settlement proposal, including the peacekeeping force and postsettlement
reconstruction aid.

Neither ASEAN nor its friends, including the United States, are trying to bleed Vietnam. Humanitarian assistance to the Vietnamese people has continued from many quarters. It would be wrong, however, for the world community to continue normal relations of trade and assistance with Vietnam as long as it continues to occupy Cambodia.

If Hanoi is determined to continue its occupation of Cambodia regardless of the price it pays, economic and diplomatic pressure will not prevent it from doing so. The denial of trade and assistance by the West does, however, impose a cost on Vietnam in terms of benefits foregone and presents it with a clear choice. Hanoi, by its policies, can choose between the continued military occupation of its neighbor and normal relations with the rest of the world. The benefits Vietnam could derive from expanded trade and other contacts with the West and ASEAN, if it would alter the policies that led to its isolation, are obvious.

China's Position

In invading Cambodia, Vietnam has also gained the enmity of its most powerful neighbor, China. It is ironic that China and Vietnam, countries which once described themselves as "lips and teeth," have now become bitter enemies. China, the United States, and ASEAN have a parallel interest in ending Vietnam's occupation of Cambodia through a political settlement which would also reduce Hanoi's dependence on the U.S.S.R., lessening the opportunities for an expansion of Soviet interests in the region. We, of course, have consistently made known our total abhorrence of the Khmer Rouge, whom the Chinese supported in power and continue to support. China has, however, accepted the formula of the International Conference on Kampuchea of free elections to establish a legitimate Cambodian Government. It has also publicly supported the emergence of a neutral, non-communist Cambodia after a Vietnamese withdrawal. The Chinese, like the United States and ASEAN, refuse only to accept Vietnam's domination of Cambodia.

Instead of a positive response to ASEAN's efforts, Hanoi continues to deny that there is a Cambodia problem. ASEAN's con-

cerns are dismissed as border issues amenable to resolution
through bloc-to-bloc talks between ASEAN and the Indochinese
states. Hanoi's approach is designed to draw ASEAN into open-
ended talks about peace and security in Southeast Asia, talks
which would serve to grant implicit recognition to the Heng Samrin regime. Vietnam refuses to discuss the fundamental cause of
instability in Southeast Asia—Vietnam's occupation of Cambodia.

U.S. Policy

The U.S. response to the events in Cambodia has been a deepening concern for the welfare of the Khmer people and the peace
of this important region. The Vietnamese occupation of Cambodia
is an inherently unstable situation because the Khmer people will
never willingly accept domination by Vietnam and because Hanoi's neighbors cannot accept Vietnamese expansionism and aggression—nor can we.

Our objective, which is shared widely and most notably by the
ASEAN nations whose security is most directly at stake, is a political settlement that will end Hanoi's occupation and, by free elections, return to the Khmer people the right to choose their own
leaders. Under truly free elections there is no danger that the
Khmer Rouge would regain power. That is why the formula for
a political settlement developed by ASEAN includes measures to
ensure that armed groups, including the Khmer Rouge, do not interfere in the free elections to choose a postsettlement government.
We support this approach.

Such an approach provides the opportunity for the Khmer
people to determine freely their own future; it provides security
to the other countries of Southeast Asia against the threat of new
Vietnamese aggression; it provides the key to ending Vietnam's
dangerous dependence on the Soviet Union; and for Vietnam itself, if not only offers the promise of a neutral Kampuchea that
poses no threat to Vietnam's security but it also offers the key to
development of fruitful relations with its neighbors in Southeast
Asia and with the Western industrial democracies from which all
Vietnamese would benefit.

While the United States has a strong interest in such an outcome, we recognize that the interests of others are even more vitally engaged. For the Khmer people, their own national identity is at stake and it is their efforts that will decide whether a truly national force, one free of both Vietnamese and Khmer Rouge domination, can be created. For the countries of Southeast Asia, their basic security is at stake, and it is proper that they should be the ones who take the lead—as they have—in exploring and testing Vietnamese willingness to consider a political settlement. Indeed, given our own bitter history in Indochina, no one should want to see this issue become primarily an issue between the United States and Vietnam. Such a development would only hopelessly complicate the already difficult road to a political solution.

However, the United States does have an important role to play in the search for a political solution to the tragedy of Cambodia, and we will continue to play that role:

• By continuing to make clear that Vietnam cannot have its cake and eat it too, that Vietnam must abandon its occupation of Kampuchea if it wants to have the benefits of normal relations with the United States;

• By working toward a political settlement that promises Vietnam and all the nations of the region a Cambodian Government that is not dominated by the Khmer Rouge, that is free of outside interference, and that is dedicated to growth and reconstruction within its own borders;

• By continuing to provide diplomatic and political support to the noncommunist Khmer resistance;

• By continuing to oppose Vietnamese efforts to gain international legitimacy for their puppet regime in Phnom Penh;

• By maintaining and, if necessary, increasing our security assistance to Thailand, which is now a front-line state. Indeed, in the last 4 years, U.S. security assistance to Thailand has increased more than threefold; and

• By continuing to support the humanitarian efforts of the UN Border Relief Organization and the International Committee of the Red Cross. In the fiscal year just ending, our contributions to those organizations for Kampuchean border relief totaled $11.5 million.

The Khmer resistance coalition formed in 1982 is an important part of ASEAN's efforts to find a solution in Cambodia. The United States gives diplomatic and political support to the noncommunist elements in the coalition, under Prince Sihanouk and Son Sann, which represent the genuine alternative to the Khmer Rouge under Pol Pot and those under Vietnam. Last year the President met with Prince Sihanouk and Mr. Son Sann together in New York as part of our support for their efforts to liberate Cambodia. They represent the genuine voice of the Khmer people and have an important role still to play in their country's future. We do not give weapons to any of the resistance groups. We, of course, give no aid of any kind to and have no contact with the Khmer Rouge.

Vietnam and its supporters have regularly challenged the credentials of the Cambodian delegation to the United Nations as part of its effort to seat its client regime. The United States has always joined ASEAN in opposing these challenges on the technical ground that the United Nations can withdraw credentials only if there is a superior claimant to the seat. There is no superior claimant to the Cambodian seat. The Heng Samrin regime is certainly not a superior claimant. On the other hand, to leave the Cambodian seat vacant would be to deny Cambodia, a member since 1954, its right to participate in the General Assembly and to have its voice heard. Had the United Nations followed such a formula in 1979, Prince Norodom Sihanouk would have been denied the UN platform to plead Cambodia's case to the world.

The United States will continue to support efforts designed to maintain political and economic pressure on Vietnam until it agrees to work toward an acceptable political settlement in Cambodia. Some argue we should soften our stance toward Vietnam to give it an alternative to the Soviets. However, it is not the policies of ASEAN or the United States which isolate Vietnam and leave it dependent on the Soviet Union. It is Hanoi's own policy of invading and occupying a neighbor which leaves it without friends outside the Soviet camp. Only a change in those policies will allow Hanoi to expand its contacts with the rest of the world.

We cannot consider an improvement in U.S.-Vietnamese relations as long as Hanoi continues to occupy Cambodia. Normalization of relations between the United States and Vietnam will require a settlement in Cambodia, as well as substantial progress and cooperation on accounting for Americans missing from the war in Indochina. Our interests in ASEAN and the strong feelings of the American people would permit nothing less.

The search for peace in Cambodia is still far from fruition, primarily because of Hanoi's intransigence and its determination to control Cambodia. It will not be easy to persuade Hanoi that an acceptable settlement in Cambodia is the only lasting solution to the instability in Southeast Asia. ASEAN, backed by the world community, has established a viable framework for a settlement. It is Hanoi which rejects all compromise.

A political settlement will be possible only once Vietnam realizes the disastrous results its policies have produced. Only a change in Hanoi's policy will reconcile Vietnam's interests with those of its neighbors and bring peace to the region. Until then, the international community must continue to maintain the pressure on Vietnam.

The world has many problems and other crises, other atrocities have driven Cambodia from the front pages. But in Cambodia, the dying, the suffering of those who have sought refuge along the Thai-Cambodian border, and the slow strangling of Khmer culture and society continue. The world cannot afford to forget Cambodia and leave the Khmer people to whatever cruel fate history and Hanoi devise for them. And the Cambodian people, who ask only to be left in peace, deserve better of the world.

SITUATION IN KAMPUCHEA[4]

A principal purpose of this United Nations is to preserve the right to self-determination, independence, security, and sovereignty of all nations. The Charter is clear, so is the history of the Unit-

[4]Reprint of a statement before the United Nations General Assembly (Oct. 30, 1984) by former U. S. Representative to the United Nations Jeane J. Kirkpatrick. *Department of State Bulletin.* 85: 57–58. Ja. '85. Copyright © 1985 by the U. S. Department of State. Reprinted by permission.

ed Nations in emphasizing and encouraging self-determination and independence of nations. The United Nations can, indeed, be proud of its role in advancing self-determination for millions of people and in working to preserve the independence of all nations. There is no principle that was more widely shared or more basic than that one nation should not use force to invade and subjugate another people.

The people of Cambodia, however, continue in occupation by a foreign power, denied their right to self-determination and independence by the Socialist Republic of Vietnam, which invaded and continues illegally to occupy Cambodia. Five times the world community has called on Vietnam to withdraw its illegal expeditionary force and to restore to the Khmer people their right to seek their own destiny under a freely chosen government without outside interference. The overwhelming margins which have supported the General Assembly's call for withdrawal of foreign forces reflect the concern of the great majority of the world's nations at the continuing tragedy in Cambodia.

What has occurred in the wake of these resolutions? Hanoi, aided and abetted by the Soviet Union, ignores those resolutions, continuing its illegal occupation of Cambodia and its oppression of the Cambodian people in violation of the Charter of the United Nations and in defiance of the expressed will of the General Assembly, offering to the Cambodian people no opportunity for self-determination or self-government. The need to address the situation in Cambodia for the sixth time is testimony to the stubborn policy of military conquest and colonization being pursued by the Socialist Republic of Vietnam.

During the past two decades, Cambodia's people have endured unmatched suffering. Hanoi's use of Cambodian territory in its war against the South and the war between the Khmer Republic and the Communist Khmer Rouge, aided by Hanoi, destroyed Cambodia's economy. Khmer Rouge victory in 1975 brought a horror the world still struggles to comprehend. Systematic political murder and starvation took the lives of more than 1 million Cambodians and nearly destroyed an ancient culture.

The Socialist Republic of Vietnam must bear a full measure of responsibility for the tragic tyranny of the Khmer Rouge. Vietnam's support was critical to the Khmer Rouge victory in 1975. Hanoi's claim that it invaded Cambodia to liberate the Khmer people from Pol Pot and that it remains there only to prevent his return to power is a transparent deception. Vietnam deposed Pol Pot only when it became apparent that it could not dominate and control the Khmer Rouge. No one laments the demise of the Khmer Rouge, a regime detested universally. But Hanoi did not invade Cambodia for the purpose of returning Cambodia to its people. Instead, Vietnam did so in order to install a puppet regime largely comprising former followers of Pol Pot, including the hated Heng Samrin himself.

Now, the Cambodian people are threatened with the loss of their homeland and the extinction of their culture. Thousands of Vietnamese nationals have settled throughout Cambodia, abetted and encouraged by Hanoi. Independent observers have estimated their number to exceed 500,000. Vietnam's clients in Phnom Penh have been instructed to assist Vietnamese, both former residents and new immigrants, in any way possible and to consult with their Vietnamese superiors before taking any action affecting Vietnamese settlers. Vietnamese immigrants are also given extraterritorial status and many have reportedly received Cambodian citizenship. This officially sanctioned Vietnamese immigration raises serious questions about Hanoi's long-term intentions toward Cambodia. It will be the ultimate tragedy if Cambodia, decimated by war and famine, should now be extinguished as an entity, overrun, submerged, and colonized by its expansionist neighbor.

Nearly 250,000 Khmer civilians remain encamped along the Thai-Cambodian border, unable or unwilling to return to their homes. Assistance to them remains an international responsibility. The United States will continue to do its share and urges other nations to continue their support for this program of humanitarian assistance. We offer our sincere appreciation to the Secretary General and his Special Representative for Humanitarian Assistance to the Kampuchean People Dr. Tatsuro Kungi for their efforts on behalf of the Khmer people uprooted by invasion and war. The staffs of the UN border relief operation, the World Food Program, the UN High Commissioner for Refugees, and other specialized UN agencies, the International Committee of the Red

Cross, and the various voluntary organizations continue their important and untiring work in providing emergency food and medical care to the displaced Cambodian people, often under dangerous conditions caused by Vietnamese attacks. Their efforts have earned the commendations of the international community and our admiration. Special thanks are also due to the Royal Thai Government for its aid to the Khmer people, particularly during the fighting earlier this year.

Vietnam's invasion and occupation of Cambodia is a challenge to the UN system and to the international community. The challenge is to induce Vietnam to withdraw its army and to restore Cambodia's independence, sovereignty, and neutrality without permitting a return to power of the Khmer Rouge. The members of the Association of South East Asian Nations (ASEAN) have provided the world the leadership to meet the challenge here at the United Nations and beyond.

The 1981 UN-sponsored International Conference on Kampuchea, in its final declaration, worked out the principles which must guide a settlement of the Cambodian problem: a cease-fire and withdrawal of all foreign forces under UN supervision; free elections under international auspices; and arrangements to ensure that armed groups do not interfere in free elections and respect the results of those elections. Ninety-four nations participated in that conference. Its principles have been endorsed by five successive resolutions of the General Assembly. They provide the best basis for meeting the challenge posed by the Cambodia crisis. The United States supports these principles and extends its appreciation to Mr. Willibald Pahr, Chairman of the International Conference on Kampuchea, and to Ambassador Massamba Sarre and his colleagues of the *ad hoc* committee for their continuing efforts in seeking a settlement in Cambodia.

The United States affirms its support for Mr. Pahr's recent proposal to internationalize the temple complex surrounding Angkor Wat so that these ruins can be restored free from danger of war. Mr. Pahr's proposals merit international support. The ruins at Angkor Wat and Angkor Thom represent the greatest achievements left by classical Khmer civilization and are a cultural treasure of importance to the entire world. Their destruction through neglect and war would be a tragic loss to us all. Despite political concerns, the ASEAN nations have endorsed Mr. Pahr's initiative. Unfortunately, Phnom Penh and its Vietnamese masters have denounced the proposal. It is not surprising that Hanoi shows no interest in preserving these relics of Cambodia's glorious cultural heritage. But it is sad that Hanoi's Cambodian clients are unable to assert enough independence even to save the enduring symbol of Khmer civilization.

Vietnam, unfortunately, rejects the reasonable proposals of the ICK (the International Conference on Kampuchea), insisting that the situation in Cambodia is irreversible. ASEAN has sought to work out the framework of a settlement which preserves the legitimate security concerns of Cambodia's neighbors, including Vietnam, as long as the key elements of Vietnamese withdrawal and free elections are preserved. The September 1983 ASEAN "Appeal for Kampuchean Independence" proposed a territorially-phased Vietnamese withdrawal, coupled with an international peacekeeping force and reconstruction aid in the area vacated, as part of a Vietnamese commitment to a complete withdrawal and elections. Hanoi rejects this proposal, insisting that it will maintain its clients in Phnom Penh for as long as necessary until the world finally accepts its domination of Cambodia. Hanoi ultimately seeks, then, the legitimization of its client regime.

But that regime clearly does not represent the Cambodian people and its pretensions to do so have been repeatedly rejected by the people of Cambodia, by its neighbors and by the General Assembly. Vietnam no longer offers its clients as claimants to Cambodia's seat at this Assembly. Their regime remains dependent on Vietnamese soldiers and Vietnamese officials to remain in place. The growing appeal of the nationalist organizations led by Prince Norodom Sihanouk and former Prime Minister Son Sann is indicative of the fact that the Khmer people are unwilling to accept a regime established on the bayonets of a foreign army. The United States welcomes the presence in this debate of Prince Sihanouk and Son Sann. They and the organizations they lead are the true embodiment of Khmer nationalism and the hopes of Cambodians for a future which is neither Khmer Rouge nor Vietnamese.

To what lengths will Vietnam's rulers go to impose their will on others? The war in Cambodia, and the confrontation with China it has engendered, have drained Vietnam's economy. With a per capita income far lower than any of its ASEAN neighbors, indeed, one of the lowest in the world, Vietnam supports the world's third largest standing army. Unable to pay the costs itself, Vietnam has turned increasingly to the Soviet Union for assistance. Massive Soviet aid meets Hanoi's military needs but cannot meet the needs of the Vietnam people, thousands of whom have risked their lives to flee in small boats rather than remain in a Vietnam oppressed and destitute. Other nations have reduced their aid because of their opposition to Vietnam's occupation of Cambodia. Moscow has traded on its aid to increase its military presence in Vietnam, establishing now a major air and naval base at Cam Ranh Bay and underlining the falseness of Vietnam's claim to be a nonaligned nation.

Even Vietnam's rulers have begun to realize that their efforts to control Cambodia have failed and that they face an increasingly difficult situation. In recent months Hanoi has tried to demonstrate to the world its willingness to reach a political settlement. In speeches and interviews, the Vietnamese Foreign Minister has hinted at Hanoi's willingness to negotiate a settlement at a conference and its willingness to consider peacekeeping activities in Cambodia.

Genuine Vietnamese willingness to negotiate a settlement in Cambodia based upon the principles of the International Conference on Kampuchea and successive resolutions of the United Nations would be a welcome development, above all, for the Cambodian people. But Hanoi apparently still views a political settlement simply as a means, one more tactic, to legitimize its client regime and secure it against the threat from the Cambodian resistance. Then, Vietnam says, it will withdraw the "bulk" of its army. The world rejects this concept of a settlement and will continue to reject it.

It should be noted that Vietnam put on its "peace mask" in March of this year during its Foreign Minister's trip to Indonesia and Australia. Days after his return to Hanoi, the Vietnamese Army launched its dry season offensive along the Thai-

Cambodian border. In March and April of this year, Vietnamese forces launched a series of assaults, backed by armor and heavy artillery, against the civilian encampments, there forcing more than 80,000 people to flee to safety inside Thailand. Nearly 50,000 of these civilians still remain in temporary encampments, unable to return because of the ever-present threat of Vietnamese shelling or attack. Even as Hanoi talks of a settlement and negotiations today, the Vietnamese Army is building up its forces near Thailand, threatening the civilian encampments which house 250,000 Cambodians. New units have moved up near the border and artillery fire continues to threaten the residents of these camps. It is an ominous harbinger for the coming dry season, which may begin only after this General Assembly completes its work. The world will mark Vietnam's actions in Cambodia as well as hear its words.

In time, the Cambodians' quiet, heroic determination will convince its leaders that they cannot subjugate the Khmer people. We hope that realization will lead to a settlement of the Cambodia problem to the satisfaction of all parties, most importantly the Cambodian people. The way to a fair and just settlement has been shown by the international community. The General Assembly resolutions on Cambodia, the 1981 International Conference on Kampuchea, and ASEAN's "Appeal for Kampuchean Independence" all outline a basis for a comprehensive settlement of Cambodia involving complete withdrawal of foreign forces, UN-supervised free elections and nonintervention and noninterference in Cambodia internal affairs. Such a settlement would guarantee a free and neutral Cambodia and constitute a threat to none of its neighbors. It would also end Vietnam's international isolation, restore Vietnam's dignity and freedom of action and permit Vietnam to turn to the task of building its own economy and uplifting the living conditions of the long-suffering Vietnamese people.

The United States looks forward to that day, and in the meanwhile, offers its full support to the efforts of the Secretary General and his representatives, to the ASEAN countries and, above all, to the people of Cambodia in their struggle.

III. VIETNAM VETERANS' MEMORIAL IN WASHINGTON AND THE POWs

EDITOR'S INTRODUCTION

The third section of this volume turns to the aftermath of the war in the United States. Much has been written of the Vietnam generation and its adjustment to a postwar world, but within recent times the Vietnam veterans have been the object of particular attention. In the autumn of 1982 they were belatedly honored with a Veterans' Memorial in Washington, D. C., which has been one of the most-visited of the capital's monuments. The monument consists of a stark, V-shaped wall of shining black granite, on which the names of the 58,000 American servicemen who died in Vietnam are inscribed. It refrains from making any political statement, yet its impact on those who have visited it has been profound and moving. The memorial is a measure of the new esteem being accorded the Vietnam veterans despite the controversies still surrounding the war itself. America's POWs and MIAs are now also receiving renewed attention. But although President Reagan has called the recovery of the soldiers missing in Vietnam "the highest national priority," their recovery—if indeed there are any POWs still in Indochina—remains in the gravest doubt.

Section III begins with a series of articles about the Veterans' Memorial. The first of these, by Kurt Andersen, is reprinted from *Time* magazine; it describes the National Salute to the Viet Nam Veterans in Washington and the ceremonies at the memorial. It is followed by an editorial from the *New Republic* that regards the war as a tragedy of American foreign policy but concedes that the monument is "one of the most impressive memorials" they have seen. David A. Hoekema, writing in *Commonweal,* sees in the memorial a new coming of age in America, a recognition of moral complexity. In a following article from *Commonweal,* a similar point of view is presented by Frank McConnell, who regards the true meaning of the Vietnam memorial as the psychic

wounding suffered by the nation in its loss of innocence. The concluding articles in this section deal with the troubling issue of the
POWs and MIAs. In an article from *USA Today,* Ann Martin
reviews the history of the effort to recover missing soldiers or their
remains from Vietnam. A final, sobering article by James Rosenthal, reprinted from the *New Republic,* regards the Reagan administration's exploitation of this issue as a cruel awakening of
hope for POW families. Every credible source of evidence, he concludes, indicates that there are no Americans alive in Vietnam.

A HOMECOMING AT LAST[1]

One man knelt, cried for a minute and left behind his campaign medals: Purple Heart, Bronze Star, Legion of Merit. Another, like many of the veterans in olive drab, added his name to
an *ad hoc* battalion sheet someone had staked in the ground; he
stood back, saluted, saw his reflection in the polished black stone,
then let out a kind of agonized whimper before two buddies led
him away. An Illinois mother ran her fingers once, twice across
the name JERRY DANAY, who was killed by a rocket. "It makes me
feel closer," Helen Danay said as she remembered her son.

They came like pilgrims, bigger crowds each day, to Washington's newest and most unorthodox monument: the Viet Nam Veterans Memorial. Its long walls, inscribed with the names of 57,
939 killed or missing in America's last war, are simple, elegant
and dignified, everything the Viet Nam War was not. By the end
of last week the adjacent ground was a fringe of private memorial
icons: messages in ink and gold glitter, photographs, candles, tiny
flags and hundreds of flowers. Virginian Larry Cox, one of four
survivors from a 27-man platoon, found the black granite chilling.
Still, he said, "it's a first step to remind America of what we did."

Cox was one of 15,000 veterans who made their way to the
capital last week for the National Salute to Viet Nam Veterans,

[1]Reprint of an article by Kurt Andersen, staff writer. *Time.* 120:44–46. N. 22, '82. Copyright © 1982
by *Time.* Reprinted by permission.

an event organized by the ex-soldiers for themselves. The gathering sometimes seemed conventional: patriotic eulogies, American Legion caps, martial music and maudlin, affectionate reunions of old platoon chums. But the convocation had an edge, a sense of catharsis, mainly because it was large and public. In the end, with a splendidly ragtag march down Constitution Avenue and the dedication of the Veterans Memorial, the spectacle seemed like the national homecoming the country had never offered.

Until recently, acknowledging Viet Nam veterans in such showy fashion would have connoted approval of the nightmarish war. However, "within the soul of each Viet Nam veteran," says Max Cleland, who lost both legs and a forearm in the war and headed the Veterans Administration under Jimmy Carter, "there is probably something that says, 'Bad war, good soldier.'" Their fellow Americans are only now coming to appreciate that distinction and, as Cleland says, "separate the war from the warrior." Mike Mullings of Bethany, Okla., a medic in Viet Nam, agrees that "things are changing. It might sound corny, but people have become a little more caring. It feels pretty good."

The last time so many people converged on Washington, all with Viet Nam on their minds, was to condemn the war and the U.S. Government. Then, as now, many of the visitors wore blue jeans, beards and long hair. Thirteen years ago this month at the antiwar March Against Death, the demonstrators invented a perfect piece of moral theater by reciting, one at a time, the names of 40,000 Americans who had been killed up to then. Last Wednesday morning, in a chapel at Washington's National Cathedral, the bleak recitation began again, and it seemed all the more powerful. There was now a final tally; most of the 230 readers had friends or kin among the dead, and a complicated sadness had replaced the agitprop bitterness of November 1969. David DeChant, 35, former Marine Corps sergeant who spent 31 months in Viet Nam, started with the A's: "David Aasen, Jose Abara, Richard Abbate . . . " The spare eulogy took the better part of three days, 1,000 names an hour, with only a few hours respite each morning. One reader was Caroline Baum, 26, a Quaker from Syracuse, N.Y. Said she after her 25 minutes at the altar: "Whether you believe in war or not, you should honor the dead who fought in it."

For 20 minutes, from Burd to Burris, Ronald and Nancy Reagan sat in the chapel. To the dismay of some veterans, it was the President's only participation in the week's salute, and on his way out of the chapel, he could not resist putting an ideological point on the proceedings: "We are beginning to appreciate that they were fighting for a just cause."

Indeed, for all the deliberate notes of reconciliation, politicized discord swirled around the centerpiece of the week's events: the Veterans Memorial. Three years ago, Labor Department Bureaucrat Jan Scruggs, a former Army corporal, decided that he and his fellow Viet Nam veterans needed palpable, permanent recognition in Washington, their own monument in the city of monuments. His Viet Nam Veterans Memorial Fund (V.V.M.F.) persuaded Congress to assign them two acres on the Mall, got 500,000 donors to give $7 million and managed to attract 1,421 entries to a professionally judged design competition. V.V.M.F. wanted a "reflective and contemplative" memorial with an "emphasis . . . on those who died"—including a display of their names—and "without political or military content." Maya Ying Lin, then a Yale architecture student, won the competition with her subtle, somber design, which looks like manicured stone ramparts: two angled walls, each 250 ft. long, sloping down into the ground from a height of 10 ft. at their junction. The carved names of the dead begin and end at the apex, arranged in the order of their deaths from 1959 to 1975.

Not everyone likes the memorial. For more than a year, some have snarled that its blackness and abstract unorthodoxy make it a humiliating antiwar mockery. "Too bad it wasn't a simple war," says Scruggs wearily. "Then we could put up a heroic statue of a couple of Marines and leave it at that." (Indeed, next year, to satisfy the critics, a flag and statue of three Viet Nam foot soldiers will be implanted nearby.) Virginia Veteran Jim Borland saw the memorial on Veterans Day and found it "full of ambivalence," like the country's attitude toward the war.

Most who visited the quasi-underground memorial last week had simpler, visceral reactions. Said former Marine David Zien of Medford, Wis.: "My chest was hollow, and I was a bit limp. It just overwhelms you." Friends and kin looked for names, aided by roving guides carrying alphabetized directories. Minerva Peyton said she had come from Elsah, Ill., to "honor my son," dead for twelve years. She visited National Cathedral on Friday at 3 a.m. to hear William Peyton's name, and she liked the severe granite memorial. "It's not ostentatious," she said. Nearly everyone ran their hands over the carved letters of familiar names.

V.V.M.F. Chairman Jack Wheeler, a West Point graduate and Yale-educated lawyer, thinks the memorial, discomforting or not, marks a turning point. Says he: "It exposes, and thereby ends, the denial that has characterized the country's reaction to the war. It is probably," he ventures, "the single most important step in the process of healing and redemption."

But the week in Washington was not all gravely introspective. In Georgetown restaurants and funky taverns, the war's survivors celebrated that survival. The lobby of the Sheraton Washington Hotel, for instance, was turned into a sort of nonstop cash-bar bivouac. Hundreds of vets, mainly Army, swarmed and shouted ("Airborne? Whoa!") with drinks in hand.

One room upstairs at the Sheraton was close and smoky, the emotional tone jangly. Here was a weeper, there a grinning josher, and everywhere beer bottles and nervous wives. For the two dozen former Special Forces men jammed into the hotel suite for their reunion, many dressed in fatigues, there had clearly never been a Veterans Day quite like this. "How are the Green Berets different?" piped up former Sergeant Mark Atchison. Tougher? Smarter? No. "We believed it. We tried to win their hearts and minds. We never called 'em 'gooks.'" An instant later at the bar an argument about a shoulder patch turned into an abortive brawl. "A lot of people here," suggested Russ Lindley, a long-haired ex-paratrooper, "are letting it out for the first time."

There was a curious pastiche of a show at Constitution Hall, almost as confused as the war. Jimmy Stewart read a letter from the fatherless son of a Viet Nam casualty, Carol Lawrence recited *The Story of the Battle Hymn of the Republic,* and erstwhile Starlet Chris Noel recreated the Armed Forces Radio show she had broadcast to U.S. servicemen in Indochina during the 1960s. During intermission, retired General William Westmoreland, commander of U.S. forces in Viet Nam from 1964 to 1968, signed autographs. The hardest working star was Wayne Newton, who flew in from Las Vegas and performed gratis. For 90 minutes, he played the banjo and trumpet, sang soul songs and *Danke Schön,* danced and winked. Said one Wisconsin vet: "I wouldn't have picked Wayne Newton. But I don't know why we're here either."

Saturday's three-hour parade down Constitution Avenue, led by Westmoreland, was the vets' own show. The 15,000, in uniforms and civvies, walked among floats, bands and baton twirlers. The flag-waving crowds even cheered.

Around the country, in fact, Viet Nam veterans sense a growing acceptance, an accommodation that owes more to plain human respect and less and less to pity. Washington's is not not the only monument. Last week in downtown Chicago a commemorative fountain was dedicated, and in Vermont, Interstate 89 last month became Viet Nam Veterans Memorial Highway. On the courthouse lawn in Glasgow, Ky. (pop. 13,000), the brand new black granite marker is still awaiting the names of Barren County's two dozen Viet Nam dead.

"Viet Nam veterans," says Stan Horton, a former Marine pilot, "used to be like cops—no one was comfortable around us. People are now more willing to listen." Horton is director of the Houston chapter of the Viet Nam Veterans Leadership Program (V.V.L.P.), which was founded with a modest Government grant last year to foster self-helping voluntarism among the vets. The main goals: to get one another jobs and burnish their collective reputation. "There's a degree of enlightenment now on the part of employers," says Stewart Roth, supervisor of veterans's job programs for California. "They're coming around." Only a small fraction of the war's veterans, after all, came home with serious emotional problems, even though for a decade the Viet Nam veteran has been portrayed in films and on TV as a doped-up maniac itching to mow down strangers. More and more, says Horton, the public is "seeing vets not as baby killers but, at worst, as dupes—and, at best, as people who did their patriotic duty." Yet the veterans remain wary. "The shift America's mood is a subtle one," says Steve Bailey, a Houston doctor and volunteer counselor of Viet Nam veterans. "The vets I talk to are waiting to see if the feeling endures past Armistice Day."

For many veterans, sheer good will is not good enough. Larry Hill, an unemployed former Marine from the Watts district of Los Angeles, derides last week's affair in Washington as "a pacification tactic." In New York City's Bedford-Stuyvesant neighborhood, itself a combat zone, Larry Smith is equally acid: "We don't need that statue. We need some jobs." He lost his left leg in Viet Nam, and he believes he was contaminated by the defoliant Agent Orange.

A tiny minority of Viet Nam veterans were exposed to Agent Orange. Yet the Veterans Administration's handling of the issue has ranged from indifferent to slipshod, and serves for the veterans as a vivid example of Government callousness. Dioxin, the toxic ingredient in Agent Orange, has been linked with skin diseases, birth defects and cancer. Yet, according to reports last month by both the General Accounting Office and the Office of Technology Assessment, the VA has been inexcusably reluctant to study the effects of Agent Orange and has provided only cursory, inadequate medical exams for the 95,000 men who have asked to be tested. The VA has also refused to pay any disability benefits on grounds of Agent Orange exposure.

The Reagan Administration this year proposed cutting $328 million from Viet Nam veterans' benefit programs, including all money for Operation Outreach under which more than 100 storefront centers have been opened to provide counseling for troubled vets. "Americans may be changing their feelings about vets," concedes Tom Liddell, a Houston attorney and former Air Force captain, "but the change in mood is not going to affect the vets until people put money where their mouths are."

Fifty years ago last summer, the "Bonus Army" of World War I veterans gathered in Washington during the Depression and vainly demanded a lump-sum payment 13 years before it was due. Like the Bonus Army the men (and 8,000 women) who served in Viet Nam want certain concrete considerations from their Government, particularly a full Agent Orange inquiry. They also want a far more diffuse and difficult kind of recognition: national respect. If the way they were sent to fight makes it almost impossible for Viet Nam veterans to be hailed as heroes, they are at least no longer made to feel like pariahs. One of them, DeChant, is hopeful, if not jubilant. "It's like any traumatic event," he says. "In order to really deal with it, the nation had to have some distance. Now, I think, it has got it."

WHAT'S IN A NAME?[2]

I am heading over to see the new Vietnam War memorial, and pause for a minute to watch the President's helicopter take off from the White House. It is a brilliant cold day with last of the maples fiery red around the Ellipse. A temporary lath archway just over my head says CHRISTMAS PAGEANT OF PEACE, and there is the place ready for the big national Christmas tree when the time arrives.

There is a rumble—here he comes! I can imagine the cheery warmth inside. Reagan has extricated himself without too much loss of face from his effort to impose sanctions on our allies for selling parts to Russia for the Siberian pipeline. Reporters are not vindictive; we won't rub it in. We have tacitly agreed not to heckle the President too much if he gets his policies mixed up, or his facts wrong, in his affable explanations. He has held fourteen formal White House press conferences in two years. F.D. R. had them twice a week. In London, Margaret Thatcher also holds two question periods a week. Reagan does take five minutes every Saturday to explain things on radio (without questions), and he is off overnight to Louisiana and Florida to explain his policies.

There is a mutter of engines, the big gray-green helicopter whirls over. I am standing right at Zero Milestone: "Starting point of the First Transcontinental Motor Convoy over the Lincoln Highway in VII-JVL-MCMXIX." The sun beats blindingly on the White House and its two piazzas. My, the flagstaff is high; it must be thirty feet.

[2]Reprint of an article by the editors. *New Republic.* 187:6, 39. D. 6, '82. Copyright © 1982 by the *New Republic.* Reprinted by permission.

I walk past the White House down to the Mall and the Vietnam War memorial. It is on hallowed ground—two acres of land near the Lincoln Memorial and the Washington Monument. The controversial design follows a controversial war that cost almost fifty-eight thousand lives. The war was a twenty-five year struggle to contain Communism, a war that U.S. Presidents could not afford to lose and were afraid to win. It ended in the final eerie days of spring 1975, when South Vietnam slowly collapsed like a building going down under demolition charges and the last of the besieged Americans lifted off a rooftop in a helicopter.

How do you have a memorial for this sort of thing? Seven million dollars were raised for it and the winning design was that of Maya Yang Lin, a young Yale architecture student. The contestants were instructed only that their entries display the names of the fallen "without political or military content." I think it is one of the most impressive memorials I ever saw.

It is an outdoor affair. As you approach the monument, you come up a walk bent to make a long V, each side of which is two hundred and fifty feet long. The meadow is on one side, and the polished granite slabs on the other. The slabs have names on them; they are sunk into a gentle hill. It is the names that do it. They are not listed by rank or alphabet, but in the order of their deaths. These were eager young men fighting in the jungles. Sometimes they thought they knew what they were doing; often they were confused. Now the names are there—Leland G. Deeds, Imlay S. Swiddeson, Richard M. Seng—but thake your eye off the cluster and you can't find the place again. It's just names, people, you and me, and our sons. There are no inscriptions to tell you what to think; there are no heroic utterances. It is stark. Each name is a special boy who never came home. It is all left to the observer. The dark, shining slabs of granite are as hard and polished as a mirror, and you can see your image reflected over the names as you lean forward. My eyes moistened. In the crowd we looked at each other, deeply moved.

This austere jumble is extraordinarily personal, it appears, judging by the first week's experience. In a bold, slow tone, the individual names were read in a chapel in Washington's National Cathedral, one of the ceremonies that took place to honor those who served in Vietnam. It took three days, one thousand names an hour, with only a few hours off each morning. At the memorial itself volunteers have books telling where individual names can be located. Small flags flutter at the base; at some spots a family has placed a wreath. One reads, "SP/4 Peter Lopez, A True American Hero, Eddie, Danny, Rosie, Lizbel, Mable, Mom and Dad: We miss you."

One man points at the name of Jose P. Ramos and his friend takes the picture. There is a search for names, and it will be hard to keep the place clear of trivia all saying the same thing: this is not a name, it is a person. My firend tells me of Larry Stevens (Panel No. 32-west, line 33). They chatted on an A-4 Skyhawk off the U.S.S. Coral Sea; the next day Stevens was missing. Now he is here, like those long lines of little stones in Arlington National Cemetery across the Potomac.

Some have said they think the memorial is too negative; perhaps they have spoken before seeing its powerful effect on visitors. Crowds increased each day at the memorial ceremonies. Officials agreed to add a conventional sculpture of three soldiers next year. They can do nothing, I think, to increase its impressiveness.

This was the war that marked America's coming of age. We had never lost a war before—America could not lose one! And yet we did, and the American Ambassador ignominiously flew off the roof of the United States embassy. The Indochina war lasted through the Administrations of five Presidents [sic], Roosevelt through Johnson (who was destroyed by the Tet offensive). In effect the Presidents were seeking stalemate, not an all-out military victory. But how can you achieve stalemate in what is, essentially, a civil war? The escalation of involvement centered on how to contain Communism in Vietnam.

We are still trying to contain something. President Reagan, flying about the country, is hard at it. Keep the Russians from getting pipeline supplies, shut off their trade where possible (but sell them U.S. grain), continue the missile buildup. It is still agonizingly difficult to draw the line.

A WALL FOR REMEMBERING[3]

From a distance it is scarcely visible, and the thin black line against the surrounding lawn would not draw one's attention at all were there not a constant stream of people walking slowly past it. The shape becomes more distinct as one approaches: two walls of polished black granite form a wide "V," each wall tapering to a point at its outer limit and reaching a height of ten feet at the center. The top, not the bottom, of the wall is at ground level, and at the center, where the two walls meet, the surrounding grounds have been graded into a shallow depression.

And it is at the center that the long list of names begins. Dale R. Buis, Chester N. Ovnard, Maurice W. Flurnoy, Alfons W. Bankowsky, Frederick T. Garside. . . . It was in 1959 that the first Americans died there, in a day when the name "Vietnam" hardly ever occurred in our newspapers or our conversations. Line after line, panel after panel, the names go on, their names incised in the polished stone in the order of their death or disappearance. The list jumps from the narrow point of one wall to the point of the other and continues. Finally, once again at the center, we come to the names of the last to die, in 1975: Richard Rivenburgh, Walter Boyd, Andres Garcia, Elwood E. Rumbaugh, and Richard Vande Geer. On the walls of the Vietnam Veterans Memorial stand 57,939 names, mute remembrances of the American lives snuffed out in America's longest war.

Two uniformed Vietnam veterans, among a group of Midwesterners who have come to Washington for a few days to publicize the plight of the thirteen hundred soldiers still listed as missing in action in Vietnam, walk among the vistors with a thick directory of names and their locations on the memorial. Some visitors are merely curious about the newest of Washington's hundreds of monuments, dedicated in November, 1982. Others are grieving, their eyes filling with tears when they find the name of

[3]Reprint of an article by David A. Hoekema, author and assistant professor of philosophy at St. Olaf College, Minnesota. Commonweal. 110:797-99. Jl. 15, '83. Copyright © 1983 by Commonweal. Reprinted by permission.

a husband, a father, or a son. Even those who chatter gaily as they approach fall silent for a few minutes before the somber black expanse of the memorial.

There is a certain silence in the very design of the memorial. It is set into the ground in the gardens which lie between the stately columns of the Lincoln Memorial and the aggressive skyward thrust of the Washington Monument; from the center of the Vietnam memorial, the white stone of both can be seen in reflection. Nearby stand several monuments to the dead of the Second World War, their gilded swords and marble eagles loudly proclaiming the valor of the departed.

The Vietnam memorial speaks in more modest and restrained tones, neither glorifying nor belittling the dead whom it honors. To see it we must walk into a shallow depression in the earth, to the depth of a grave. The blackness of the commemorative wall reminds us of the reality of death, of men and women punctured by bullets or shattered by mortar rounds. Yet it remembers these horrors with a quiet dignity.

Visitors have interrupted the solemn simplicity of the memorial with their gifts and gestures of remembrance. When I visited, in late December, Christmas wreaths lay along the base of the memorial, and flowers were stuck into the tiny gaps between adjacent panels. A florist's bouquet had been delivered—the soldier's name and "Vietnam Memorial" were the only address on the card—with a message of love from "Mom, Dad, Peter, Dirk, Jana, Grandpa, and Grandma." Beside a package of vending-machine cheese and crackers lay a note in a child's hand "To my angel daddy."

Beneath one panel lay a postcard from the nearby Air and Space Museum showing a Sikorsky helicopter widely used in Vietnam; no inscription provided a clue to its intent. I shuddered, remembering—as I had remembered when I saw the helicopter itself a few days earlier—Michael Herr's account in his book, *Dispatches,* of sitting beside a soldier in such a helicopter and suddenly noticing, after the chopper took rifle fire from the ground, that the soldier's uniform was stained with blood and his eyes frozen in the blank stare of death. Thousands of stories such as these,

I thought, are concealed behind the polished granite of the memorial.

It would be foolish, were it even possible, to try to prevent visitors from embellishing the memorial with their own remembrances. Indeed, the very profusion of notes, wreaths, and dying flowers suggests the importance of the monument to those whose loved ones did not return from Vietnam. Maya Lin's design for the monument, chosen from among fourteen hundred proposals, has provoked controversy ever since its selection. The Vietnam Veterans Memorial Fund, which sponsored the design competition and raised funds to build the memorial, has responded by commissioning a realistic sculpture together with a flagpole, near the memorial wall. (Early this year an alternate proposal, which would have placed both the sculpture and the flagstaff at the apex of the two walls as if they were part of the original design, was rejected.)

When I first read about this plan it seemed an unfortunate compromise with aesthetic Philistinism. But visiting the memorial changed my judgment. It would be presumptuous of me, I realized, to object to the added sculpture if it will communicate more clearly to the veterans and the bereaved of Vietnam that their sacrifice is remembered and respected. And the addition, in any case, will not diminish the powerful statement of the simple memorial wall.

Only a few hundred yards from the Vietnam memorial I sat one afternoon, at the height of the war, and listened with half a million others to impassioned speeches calling for an end to the war. Perhaps some of the other visitors had sat there too; or perhaps they had been among the supporters of that desperate defense of American interests and prestige which so deeply divided our nation.

But these differences seemed irrelevant as we stood there, canceled out not only by the passage of time but by the inescapable fact of 58,000 deaths. The names served as a reminder of who it was that bore the heaviest burden of death and bereavement. Certain first and last names, I noted, are Dutch, and I wondered whether they came from the Dutch Calvinist community in which I was raised. But names like Tommy Lee, Juan, Sammy, and

Carlos were far more common. The proportion of black men who died in Vietnam was twice as great as their proportion in the American population. At the other social extreme—if the report of another visitor to the monument is correct—not one graduate of the Massachusetts Institute of Technology is among the Vietnam dead.

In Vietnam as in nearly every war, it was the poor and uneducated who died in the place of the wealthy and educated, and the young who died to defend the policies and privileges of the old. I thought of the comment of a friend who had seen the memorial a few days before: it reminded him, he said, that war is an institution by which old men trick teenagers into killing each other.

There are many lessons we can learn by reflecting on the experience of Vietnam: that guns and sheer determination can succeed in turning an internal struggle over self-determination and nationalism into a superpower confrontation, and that some wars can be lost in dozens of different ways but cannot be won. The present administration seems bent on forgetting these lessons, deepening its involvement and hardening its ideology in Africa and Central America. We can only pray that the headlong pursuit of confrontation and military advantage will not plunge the world into a war for whose victims there will be no monuments. For the next world war which daily threatens us all—whether it erupts from direct provocation, escalation of regional wars, or mere mistake—may be over in a matter of hours, and the survivors will not honor but envy the dead.

But when we turn from the global to the personal level, there is a great deal that we can learn from those who returned alive from Vietnam. They have been forced by their war experience, and by the deeply ambivalent reception they have received on their return, to come to grips with profound moral complexities that most of us have not yet faced. As Peter Marin has written in a moving reflection published last fall in the *Nation* (Nov. 27, 1982), we find in many Vietnam veterans "a particular kind of moral seriousness which is unusual in America, one which is deepened and defined by the fact that it has emerged from a direct confrontation not only with the capacity of others for violence and brutality but also with their own culpability, their sense of their own capacity for error and excess."

The practice of war is filled with troubling contradictions—between the ideals of freedom we claim to defend and the greed of war profiteers whose interests we serve, between the unspeakable horrors of napalm and mass executions and the acts of kindness and courage which war calls forth. Perhaps it is the very awareness of these contradictions, and the sense that nothing in human experience is purely good or purely evil, that has made it so difficult for Vietnam veterans to find a place in American society.

It is not too late to learn even from those whose lives came to an abrupt end in the jungles of Vietnam. Their voices speak eloquently in the silence of two black granite walls in Washington.

A NAME FOR LOSS: MEMORIALS OF VIETNAM[4]

By the time this appears in print, we will be some months beyond the tenth anniversary of the fall of Saigon. At the time I write this, *Newsweek, Time,* Dan Rather, Tom Brokaw, and even, God help us, David Hartman and Phil Donahue have all told us that the war was a national tragedy, that it left scars on the national self-consciousness that may last for decades, and that it is a nightmare from which we can still not awaken and Blah. Blah. Blah.

But that is not the point. The tenth anniversary of the fall of Saigon does *not* matter because Saigon was *always*—and we all knew it—about to fall.

"Vietnam" is not a metaphor for arrogant national ambition, nor a key-word for misplaced national generosity, nor a code-name for national trauma. It is, simply, a name for loss.

Unlike the First, Second, and even Korean Wars, there will never be an appropriate date to celebrate the "end" of the Vietnam War, because it never really ended. For those of us who lived

[4]Reprint of an article by Frank McConnell, staff writer. *Commonweal.* 112:441–42. Ag. 9, '85. Copyright © by *Commonweal.* Reprinted by permission.

through it on the twin battlefields of Vietnam and Amerika (remember when it was spelled that way?) and, one hopes, for those who come after, the war in Vietnam is not so much a historical detail as it is a *state of consciousness*: terrifying, and like all terrifying things, humanizing.

Think about the Vietnam Monument in Washington. As originally designed, it would have been an abstract, triangular, black formation with the names of the war dead inscribed. Nothing else, and that nothing else would have been brilliant. For it would have reminded us of another great response to war, Hemingway's epochal diminution of language in the face of the carnage of World War I in *A Farewell to Arms*. There, the protagonist Frederick Henry reflects on the words we usually use to glorify war.

"Abstract words such as glory, honor, courage, or hallow were obscene," Henry says, "beside the concrete names of villages, the numbers of roads, the names of rivers, the numbers of regiments and the dates."

This is not cynicism, but a lyrically humane response to the dehumanization of war when it is fought for Grand Causes.

Of course, the V.F.W. and the American Legion protested the Vietnam Monument as designed, and insisted that there be beside it a heroic statue of a few soldiers. And, since those organizations have a rather better-organized lobby than the poets, they got their wish. Once again—as in all countries—public policy failed to keep pace with that deep level of national self-consciousness which we call, in shorthand, art.

But this time it was a little different. The photo of the flag raising at Iwo Jima or the film, *The Best Years of Our Lives*, can never become clichés because they are testaments to, icons of, a war fought for a *truly* Grand Cause (although Norman Mailer, Joseph Heller, Kurt Vonnegut, and Thomas Pynchon have all articulated the pacifist position that even *that* war, from the viewpoint of the victim, was pointless and wasteful; so, of course, did Gandhi). At least in the case of World War II, our public memorials in their grandiosity seem somehow congruent to what both Churchill and Eisenhower referred to as a "Crusade."

Vietnam was sometimes referred to as a crusade also; and the clash between those two applications of that solemn word is as jarring as the clash between the heroic/noble statuary at the Vietnam Monument and the silent, challenging black slab adjacent to it.

We thought—or wanted to think—that the war in Vietnam was the equivalent of World War II, not just ethically but strategically. One Defense Department White Paper after another insisted that this guerrilla war could be fought as if it were a conventional conflict: they were all written by a group of intellectuals we used to refer to as "McNamara's Band." LBJ, tragically trapped in a retrospective dream of FDR and the High Crusade, was reliving the epic days of 1942 the way George III, in his last days, would sometimes awaken from slumber to shout, "Are my American colonies still loyal?" And nineteen-year-old kids were dying in panic for a reason no one could quite make clear.

On the one hand, a large black slab with the names of the dead; on the other, a craggily heroic sculpture of noble young men alert in the cause of freedom. The Vietnam Monument, in its internal dissonance, is a metaphor, and maybe a perfect metaphor, for the psychic dissonance which was and is that disastrous episode.

"What I mainly remember is the noise," said a colleague of mine who flew helicopters in Nam (I wasn't there, so I don't have the right to use that phrase, but he was, so he does). Noise: you can see only one thing at a time, but you can hear everything at once. And if you do hear everything at once, and if it's loud enough, it can drive you crazy. Think about the first thing we hear in *Apocalypse Now*: the incessant pocketapocketa of the helicopters. Think about the outrageous noise level of the Vietnam scenes in *The Deerhunter*. Think about—yes—*Rambo*.

How could Francis Coppola, Michael Cimino, and even Sylvester Stallone so precisely have caught the spirit of that awful war when the V.F.W. and the American Legion so unfortunately missed it? Perhaps it has to do with the difference *between* monuments and poems, between the public consciousness as it chooses to pose itself and the cultural consciousness as it is compelled to express itself. I do not think Mr. Coppola and Mr. Stallone could bring themselves to agree on a single political issue about the war. But I know that they "do agree about the central spiritual issue of the war: in *Apocalypse Now* and *Rambo,* Vietnam is a name for loss, and a name for loss from which we must recover or die.

The great truism about Vietnam is that the veterans of that particular obscenity have not been sufficiently honored or celebrated but have rather been treated like a national blight. That is not a truism because it is false or boring; it is a truism because it is true, and because like the point of the monument, it is hard to see. The public sector has been remarkably unsuspecting of the special agony of those who fought. Even the present administration, apparently on the brink of a disastrous foray into Nicaragua—this time we get to fight *with* the guerrillas—has managed little more than platitudes, paternal back-pats, and the kind of rhetoric Hemingway found so loathsome after Chateau-Thierry.

But if the public sector has been insensitive, the private sector—the storytellers, daydreamers, musicians, and filmmakers—have guaranteed that the memory of Nam has entered into our consciousness and into the structure of our myths.

Thomas Magnum of *Magnum P.I.* is a hardboiled detective. He is one of the many godchildren of Raymond Chandler's Philip Marlowe, and a worthy descendant at that. But Marlowe fought in World War I, and carried into this world the bitter virtues of private nobility and private honor and public cynicism that were the legacy also of Hemingway and Fitzgerald. Magnum, on the other hand, fought in and was traumatized by Vietnam. And he carries into his world—our world—the sense of disorientation, of gallows humor, of cosmic insouciance, that perhaps best characterize the members of that generation: not a lost generation—as Hemingway described his people—but the generation that shrugs.

The Magnum shrug and grin, in fact, is the dramatic equivalent of the black slab monument, It is, I suggest, the entry into maturity of a nation that has heretofore assumed, with all the virtues of adolescence, that it was incapable of doing evil. Bruce Springsteen catches the tone too in "Born in the U.S.A.":

> had a brother at Khe Sanh
> Fightin' off the Viet Cong.
> They're still there, He's all gone.

Vietnam taught us to shrug—the way you shrug when you hear your cat has been run over in the street, out of recognition of the inevitability of loss—but in teaching us that, it taught us, with luck, the moral perceptions that lie behind the cosmic shrug. "Sorry about that"—the Nam phrase that covered everything from a broken latrine to a twenty-four-hour firefight—has passed into the laguage and may, rightly read, be taken as a theological perception. As in *Amen.*

Even our technological myths have been transformed by the Vietnam experience. *Rambo, Blue Thunder, Magnum P.I.,* and any number of other films and TV shows feature ex-Nam soldiers who are also involved with the technology of the helicopter. And, as Colin Westerbeck, Jr. observed in one of his brilliant reviews in *Commonweal,* the helicopter is the technological icon of the eighties: beautiful, mobile, graceful, and deeply threatening. The fighter plane, the icon of World War II and of Korea, was unidirectional, fast, and sure of purpose. The helicopter—no, the chopper—the icon of Nam, is omnidirectional, ambiguous, and capricious. It is the technology of the shrug.

But one could multiply the examples beyond endurance. The point is that the *real* memorial of Vietnam is not on a field in Washington but in the presence the war exerts on our most intimate dream lives, our popular fantasies. The Vietnam vet, to our common shame, has been largely forgotten in the economy and in our national agencies. He will not be forgotten in whatever mythologies we leave behind us, for he suffered a kind of universal coming-to-consciousness which is also a universal awakening-to-emptiness which could be the beginning (according to the Christian and Taoist mystics) of spiritual adulthood.

It can be scant consolation to those poor men suffering unemployment, delayed stress syndrome, or just bad dreams; nevertheless, it is true that no lasting culture has failed to produce an epic literature based, not on its great victory, but on its definitive defeat, from the *Iliad* to the *Song of Roland* to *The Charge of the Light Brigade.*

In our stories and dreams, Vietnam deserves and has its timeless memorial. We were there. We always will be.

FAMILIES OF VIETNAM WAR POW'S AND MIA'S:
THE ORDEAL CONTINUES[5]

The fighting has stopped and the guns are quiet, but the Vietnam War is not over. Over 2,500 prisoners and missing did not return from Southeast Asia after the signing of the Paris Peace Accords which ended official U.S. involvement in Vietnam in 1973, and the Defense Intelligence Agency continues to receive hundreds of first- and second-hand live sighting reports of Americans still being held captive in Indochina. After a decade of government repression of the issue, public and media concern has only recently been growing in light of Pres. Reagan's renewed interest and Bo Gritz's widely publicized, but unsuccessful, forays into Laos last year to rescue captive American prisoners.

The American prisoners of war were Hanoi's most valuable propaganda and bargaining tools, and the North Vietnamese government exploited the POW's to the best of its political advantage. However, the extraordinary and unprecedented manner in which the U.S. government has manipulated the POW-MIA issue for nearly 20 years and has used the families of the prisoners and missing for political gain has rarely been considered.

The POW-MIA issue has remained a significant matter of concern to every presidential administration since Lyndon Johnson, and the POW-MIA families continue to be tangled in the web of political rhetoric today. The problem proves to be one of the most unique and controversial aspects of the Vietnam War and, if the government's treatment of the prisoners of war, those missing in action, and their families for two decades is any indication of policy in future conflicts, our examination of this issue is imperative.

On Aug. 5, 1964, a U.S. Navy Skyhawk was shot down near Hanoi. The pilot, a 27-old-year Navy lieutenant who never completed his first and last mission, was quickly captured. In broad-

[5]Reprint of an article by Ann Martin, a free-lance writer. *USA Today*. 112:32–37. My. '84. Copyright © 1985 by *USA Today*. Reprinted with permission.

casts heard outside of Vietnam, Radio Hanoi announced that "the pilot, pale, weary, and awestricken, staggered along the streets of Hongay in his dirty U.S. uniform under the escort of proud Vietnamese People's Army men" and was "put on public display." Lt. Everett Alvarez, Jr., the first American prisoner of war in Vietnam, eventually spent nearly nine years as a prisoner of war in North Vietnam—approximately three times as long as any American prisoner was held during both world wars and the Korean War. By the end of the first year of American military escalation in Indochina, nearly 60 pilots had traded in their flying suits for black Vietnamese prison pajamas, and Hanoi immediately seized the opportunity to use the American prisoners for propaganda. North Vietnamese officials insisted that the POW's were "war criminals" since the U.S. had never declared war on North Vietnam, and, rather than adhering to the principles of the 1949 Geneva Agreement which protected the fundamental human rights of prisoners of war, Hanoi outraged U.S. leaders by invoking the Nuremberg doctrine which required that "individuals be responsible for war crimes, even if carried out in obedience to higher authority." The North Vietnamese threatened to try the American flyers in civil courts and, in August, 1965, two American pilots were beheaded "by order of the communist high command."

The initial reaction of the U.S. was silence. The State Department sent the North Vietnamese a formal note which expressed the government's consternation, but the Johnson Administration discouraged publicity. It was not until May and June, 1966, when captured American pilots were paraded through downtown Hanoi to the screams and abuse of an angry mob, that Pres. Johnson broke his silence. During a press conference, he censured the Vietnamese actions, calling them "deplorable" and "repulsive," and appointed Ambassador-at-Large Averill Harriman to attempt to gain international support against the Vietnamese. Photographs of the bruised and bloody pilots—their heads bowed—being herded down the Hanoi streets made headlines across the country, as leaders from scores of nations flooded Hanoi with pleas for leniency. The pressure proved to be effective. On July 24, North Vietnam Pres. Ho Chi Minh conceded, saying there was "no trial in view" for any American pilots.

The Johnson Administration was the first to discover the tremendous potential the Vietnam POW's had for eliciting public
sympathy. However, the Administration also recognized that publicity could be detrimental to the President's war plans. Quite simply, the quickest way to bring the prisoners home was to end the
war, which Johnson was not willing to do. So, once the POW crisis passed, Johnson decided that quiet diplomacy between American and North Vietnamese officials in Paris would be the U.S.
government's first official policy on the POW problem. The POW
and MIA families were warned that anything they might say or
do could potentially endanger their loved ones' lives and damage
the negotiations going on in Paris. (Lois Mills, whose son, Lt.
James Mills, disappeared in 1966, remembers that a casualty officer told them not to tell anyone—not even closest friends—about
her son's disappearance. She was assured that an "exhaustive
search" was in progress and silence was essential.) Most families,
in obedient deference to the government's authority, willingly
complied, but being told to be quiet intensified the frustration and
feeling of helplessness for other POW-MIA families. Some families wanted to do something, but the government and military adamantly opposed private family actions and publicity. One MIA
wife, Valerie Kushner, told *Life*, "I wanted to yell from the first
day, but I was told by the Army they would not only not help me,
but squelch me."

As time passed and Johnson's "quiet diplomacy" produced no
visible results, a number of POW and MIA families were growing
increasingly impatient despite the government's warning not to
make any waves. In San Diego, Mrs. Sybil Stockdale, the wife of
POW senior Naval officer James B. Stockdale, had been inviting
other POW wives to her home to exchange information and boost
moral. In 1968, Mrs. Stockdale began calling POW and MIA
wives across the country to encourage them to send telegrams and
letters to the North Vietnamese delegation in Paris, as well as
newly elected Pres. Nixon and the Secretary of State. The result
was a barrage of letters to Paris and Washington. Gradually, a
number of local, informal groups of POW wives began meeting
regularly. In February, 1969, Mrs. Stockdale sent out a form letter to POW and MIA families across the country asking whether

they would be interested in participating in "a group effort to get information about our men." Even though some families were still reluctant to participate because of government's warnings, she received hundreds of positive replies. By her indefatigable efforts, an informal organization, the National League of American Prisoners in Southeast Asia, was formed in June, 1969.

A Change in Policy

Newly elected Pres. Nixon was aware of the families' growing agitation, and in January and February, 1969, the Administration was preparing to institute a major policy change concerning the American POW's. On May 18, 1969, Defense Secretary Melvin Laird met with reporters to announce that the Administration had decided to "go public" with the POW issue in an effort to pressure Hanoi to adhere to the principles of the Geneva Agreement. Nixon's new program was to be implemented through official press conferences, speaking engagements by POW returnees, and, most importantly, by enlisting the assistance of the news media and by encouraging private organizations, individuals, and families to "participate in publicity-generating activities."

In July, 1969, Lt. Robert F. Frishman was one of three POW's released by the North Vietnamese into the custody of a group of anit-war activists. Immediately upon his return, the Department of Defense arranged a press conference. Frishman, imprisoned for 20 months in Hanoi, came home with graphic and horrifying tales of torture and deprivation in the Vietnamese prisons which received wide press coverage. The thought that America had kept quiet for four years while their men were being tortured in prison sent waves of panic among the POW families. As a result, many otherwise reluctant POW-MIA families began associating with the growing League of Families.

The drama of hundreds of American soldiers silently suffering at the hands of communists captivated the American press and public. The American Red Cross, the Junior Chamber of Commerce, *Reader's Digest,* and many other groups and organizations demonstrated their concern by initiating massive letter-writing campaigns. During the last three months of 1969, literally tons of postcards and letters were delivered to the North Vietnamese in Paris. Celebrities such as Ernest Borgnine, Jimmy Stewart, and Bob Hope donated their time to make public appearances in support of the POW's. The government issued 135,000,000 POW-MIA postage stamps and distributed stickers that said, "Have a Heart Hanoi." A UCLA campus organization, VIVA (Voices in Vital America) began selling POW bracelets—metal bands inscribed with the name and date of capture of a POW—as a gesture of concern for the prisoners. Hundreds of thousands of bracelets were sold across the country, and it became almost fashionable to wear one.

With the government's decision to publicize the POW issue, the activism of the POW-MIA families was now to the Nixon Administration's advantage. During the summer of 1969, several Pentagon officals embarked on a campaign to 45 cities in order to bring the POW-MIA families together to consolidate a national organization of families to publicize the plight of the American prisoners of war in Vietnam. Nixon met in December, 1969, with 26 POW wives, including Sybil Stockdale, and "suggested" that an official organization of families, with a professional staff directing it, be founded. The Department of Defense, which for five years had cautiously avoided the POW and MIA families, now sought to win the families' favor. The POW and MIA families received Christmas cards from the White House, record albums from the Air Force, potted plants from the Navy, and wooden plaques from the Army. The Air Force sent the families official letters of application to be in the "league" and mailed out brochures advising the families how to best handle questions from the media.

The families, elated over the government's sudden display of concern for the POW's, were eager to participate in the Nixon Administration's new program, and on May 1, 1970, nearly 3,500 people, including high-ranking military officers, Congressmen, and, most notably, Vice Pres. Spiro Agnew, attended a rally in Constitution Hall. As a highlight of the rally, Astronaut Frank Borman was officially sent off on a 25-day tour around the world to petition foreign heads of state to support the American prisoners.

The rally was a tremendous success. Nearly 1,000 POW and MIA relatives, who had been flown to the meeting in military transport aircraft, remained in Washington for the League's first national meeting. On May 28, 1970, the National League of Families of American Prisoners and Missing in Southeast Asia was officially incorporated. The League was established as a non-profit, non-partisan organization which would be financed by family contributions and private donations. The sole purpose of the League, as stated in its by-laws, was to "obtain the release of all prisoners, the fullest possible accounting for the missing, and the return of the remains of those who died." Sybil Stockdale was appointed to be the first national coordinator, and the official character of the organization was demonstrated by the immediate installation of a White House WATS line in the new League office. On July 17, 1970, Spiro Agnew presented the League with a check for $10,000 in proceeds from the sale of Agnew watches and T-shirts, which was one of the largest single contributions the League has ever received.

The National League of Families began to enjoy tremendous support from the government. Each month, the Pentagon sent out an official newsletter to all the League's members with the latest information on the POW's and MIA's. League members were frequently asked to testify before Congress, and many POW wives accompanied Pentagon and Administration officials to speaking and ceremonial engagements. Robert P. Odell, the finance director for the Republican National Committee, secretly arranged for the League to use the Committee's mailing lists to raise money for League activities.

The most intriguing indication of high-level interest in the League was evidenced by a fundraising and publicity campaign proposal received from a Washington, D.C., public relations firm. Robert R. Mullen and Co., which had handled Nixon's 1968 presidential campaign and had also helped to set up and administer the Republican National Committee's finances, proposed a publicity program that included direct mail and capital fundraising, telethons, and television commercials. The proposal was signed by a recently resigned CIA employee, Howard Hunt—the same Howard Hunt who was indicted a year later for his involvement in the Watergate scandal. The Senate Watergate investigations later revealed that Robert R. Mullen and Co. had "maintained a relationship with the CIA since its incorporation in 1959" and had been providing cover for CIA agents for years. The Mullen Co. was underbid for the League contract.

Growing Disenchantment

By the beginning of 1971, a number of the League's membership began to grumble among themselves. Since 1968, the North Vietnamese had initiated the release of nine prisoners to leaders of the anti-war movement, but the U.S. government, despite its hoopla over the POW's, could not claim it had brought home a single man. Many were beginning to resent the government for exploiting the League families to support the President's war policies. Barbara Mullen, the wife of a Marine pilot lost in Laos, refused to attend any more luncheons as a "visual aide" accompanying the Chief of Naval Operations, and Mrs. James Warner quit her position as the director of the National League of Families in Michigan, saying, "We've been used to drum up war sentiment."

In 1969, the President had revealed his secret plan to end the war—Vietnamization—but, unfortunately for the POW and MIA families, Vietnamization made no provision at all for the release and accounting of the POW's and MIA's. The families felt betrayed.

The National Advertising Council (a non-profit organization supported by advertisers, agencies, and media, which donates free time and space to advertising for the public good) announced in May, 1971, that, at the request of the White House, a massive advertising campaign focusing on the plight of the Vietnam POW's was being prepared by the State and Defense Departments, the American Red Cross, and the National League of Families. The Council had agreed to donate $25,000,000 of television air time for these ads, which would focus on the "humanitarian" side of the issue by demanding that the prisoners be treated humanely and that the prisons be opened for Red Cross inspection. Frederick Papert, the chairman of PKL Companies, a supporter of the Ad-

vertising Council, made a ruckus when he publicly complained
about the strong White House involvement in the Council's POW
campaign, and he condemned the "political motivations" connect-
ed with the ads. His disenchantment with the Advertising Council
campaign ignited disillusioned POW and MIA families, who
were tired of acquiescing to the government's demands—from
Johnson's "quiet diplomacy" to Nixon's flamboyant POW campaign. Within days, between 350 and 450 POW and MIA families split from the League to form a new organization called the
Families for Immediate Release. Breaking from the League's
standard "non-political" stance, the Families for Immediate Release advocated that the only way to secure the release of the prisoners was by ending the war, and demanding that the National
Advertising Council allow their group the same $25,000,000 of
free air time for their ads, which requested viewers to write to
Washington to insist that the war end immediately. The dispute
between the Council and the Families for Immediate Release
dragged on for months, and, when the Council was unable to clear
any of the League's ads with any of the networks, the deal failed
to materialize. The Council, which claims that it does not get involved with controversial issues, was somewhat stunned by the
controversy. One of the Council's spokesmen later remarked that
"there had not been a counter-campaign to anything they prepared for a quarter of a century."

In October, 1971, Nixon made a surprise visit to the League's
annual meeting at the Statler Hotel in Washington, D.C. Although his presence was meant to remind the League of his unfal-
tering concern for the POW's, the patience of more League
families was beginning to wear thin. Signs of dissension within the
usually well-behaved League were clearly evident. Nearly 50 determined POW wives picketed the White House wearing buttons
saying "POW-MIAs Number One, not Thieu," and loyal League
members began arguing for the League to take a more "political
stance" by criticizing the Nixon Administration. However, the
League feared losing its tax-exempt status by becoming "partisan"
and the majority voted against the resolution.

News of Nixon's decision to step up naval and aerial bom-
bardment and mining operations in response to North Vietnam's

April, 1972, offensive disturbed the League, which feared that military escalation would prolong the prisoners' captivity. Approximately 300 League members gathered in Washington again in May, 1972, for a symposium. This time, the mood was overwhelmingly critical of the Administration, and a strongly worded resolution expressing the League's "extreme distress at the failure of the Administration's policy" was unanimously passed. Fifty League members paraded to the White House to deliver a letter to the President demanding a face-to-face meeting with League representatives. Both Nixon and his National Security aide, Henry Kissinger, met on May 16 with three League leaders to reiterate their concern and commitment to the POWs, and explained that, until the prisoners were released, the U.S. would not be able to terminate the daily bombings or the mining operations.

The election year afforded the League much greater lobbying power, because Nixon, in his campaign for reelection, was in no position to alienate any group—particularly one which not only elicited strong public sympathy, but had also been cultivated by his own Administration. However, the welfare of the prisoners was not the government's primary concern. A perceptive Oct. 9, 1972 *Newweek* article, "Battle of the POW's," clearly outlined the fundamental motive behind the Nixon Administration's POW propaganda war:

The President's decision to make the release of the prisoners the linchpin of American policy in Vietnam was prompted by more than his desire to win the men's freedom. Mr. Nixon was elected on a pledge to end the war, but he has been unable to do so. . . . He has steadfastly refused to withdraw U.S. support from the Government of South Vietnam president—Nguyen Van Thieu—a condition Hanoi says is essential to end the war. That being the case, Mr. Nixon needed a domestically persuasive rationale for the continued American involvement in Indochina—and the contrived loss of American lives. The POWs became that rationale. (p. 25)

On Jan. 17, 1973, Henry Kissinger signed the Paris Peace Accords, which officially ended the U.S.'s involvement in the Vietnam War. The POW and MIA families were elated that their ordeal was finally going to be over. Between February and April, nearly 600 POW's were released. However, the end of the war brought only bitter disappointment for the families of 2,500 prisoners and missing who did not return from Southeast Asia. For these families, the nightmare continued.

There were 2,553 military and 41 civilian Americans unaccounted for after the return of the final group of POW's. Of these, the Department of Defense was aware of nearly 200 unrepatriated prisoners who were either identified by the enemy by name, or by released POW's, or were known to be captive through reliable intelligence sources. Although the war was over, the POW-MIA crisis was far from over. The POW-MIA families were convinced that live Americans were still captive in Southeast Asia and desperately hoped that the U.S. government would take appropriate actions to account for the missing POW's and MIA's.

Status Reclassification

According to the Missing Persons Act of 1942, a serviceman is subject to a status review after he has been missing for one year. The resolution committee could retain his MIA status or change it to "killed in action," which was authorized if there was conclusive evidence that the man was dead, or if a "sufficient" length of time had passed without news about the person. In the latter case, a "presumptive finding of death (PFD)" was declared. Immediately after the signing of the Paris Accords, the Defense Department announced that it was "in the process of setting up resolution boards to determine the status of the MIAs." One month later, the Director of POW-MIA Affairs at the Pentagon, Brigadier Gen. Russel C. Ogan, declared that "up to 200 MIAs had alread been reclassified as dead." To the shock of the POW and MIA families, the Pentagon disclosed four days later that, within one year, all MIA's would be given presumptive findings of death.

The families were enraged that the government so willingly abandoned any live prisoners by declaring them dead. What they failed to understand was that, whether or not any prisoners were still captive in Vietnam, Laos, or Cambodia, the Defense Department's status change policy was standard procedure. In effect since March 7, 1942, the Missing Persons Act was enacted primarily to enable the Pentagon to clear its records. Most of the 11, 404 soldiers missing after World War II were lost over water and had virtually no chance of survival. It was necessary for the Department of Defense to presume each man dead in order to wipe the slates clean. Despite the fact that very few men were missing over water in Vietnam, and the Missing Persons Act was sadly outdated under the present circumstances, the Pentagon was merely following precedent.

Standard protocol or not, the POW and MIA families furiously protested the status reclassifications, claiming that men were presumed dead without sufficient evidence. In July, 1973, five families filed a class action suit (*McDonald vs. McLucas*) which was successful in obtaining a temporary injunction against MIA reclassifications until a New York District Court ruled in 1974 that the status reviews were indeed constitutional.

The families were appalled that the U.S. government, which had made the POW-MIA issue one of primary public significance and had been the catalyst in the formation of the League itself, now wanted to bury the issue. During the prior four years, the government had found that the POW's made good propaganda. The National League of POW-MIA Families was profitable to the Nixon Administration, but, when the war ended, evidently so did the League's usefulness, and at this point the government's attitude toward the League soured. As the League pursued the issue with dogged persistance, Washington's strong disapproval soon turned into a campaign to discredit the League. Washington officials publicly labelled League members as "rumor-mongers, charlatans, and profiteers" and "professional MIA celebrities." Other officials accused the League families of trying to retain their men's POW and MIA status in order to collect their pay. Almost immediately, the word spread that the National League of Families was *persona non grata* and, within a few months, contributions to the League declined tremendously.

Pres. Gerald Ford, while insisting that no American prisoners were still alive in Southeast Asia, claimed to be dedicated to obtaining a full accounting of the missing, but this prospect was unlikely becasue of his hardline politics toward the newly formed Socialist Republic of Vietnam (SRV). Article 21 of the Paris Peace Accords made clear that the U.S. was obligated to "contribute to healing the wounds of war and to postwar reconstruction." Nixon had also sent a secret letter to Pham Van Dong which promised between $3,250,000,000 and $4,750,000,000 in economic aid over a period of five years "without political conditions." Vietnam, in a shambles, was desperate for economic aid, and, in 1976, Deputy Foreign Minister Phan Hien said that Vietnam was prepared to "talk with the United States on the search for the missing American servicemen and the U.S. commitment to grant Vietnam economic aid."

As an expression of their willingness to pursue a settlement, the Vietnamese released the names of 12 U.S. pilots who had died in air crashes. Ford responded that the U.S. could not be satisfied with such "limited action" by the Vietnamese because they still had information on hundreds of other men. During the Paris talks between U.S. and SRV officials the Vietnamese, reaching desperation, essentially abandoned their hopes for reparations and asked the U.S. to agree to "costless" reconstruction through international bank loans. The Vietnamese offered to give a full MIA report and requested that diplomatic relations be established. In another "conciliatory initiative," Vietnam released information on 22 more MIA's. Although the compromise was clearly on the Vietnamese side, the U.S. remained intransigent. As one UN observer noted, "the only obstacle to the solution of the question of U.S servicemen missing in action is the Ford Administration's hostile policy."

During a televised campaign debate in October, 1976, Jimmy Carter claimed that one of the most "embarrassing failures" of the Ford Administration was that he did not send a presidential commission to Vietnam. One month after his inauguration, Carter announced that he was arranging to send an executive commission to Indochina headed by Leonard Woodcock, the president of the United Auto Workers. For four days, the five-member commission met with the Vietnamese and Laotian representatives in Hanoi and Vientiane. Again, the Vietnamese clearly expressed "strong interest in receiving aid from the United States." Pres. Carter was in favor of normalizing relations with Vietnam, and the SRV, encouraged by Carter's positive position, highlighted the commission's visit by agreeing to give the U.S. all available information on MIA's as it was found and to return the remains of missing Americans as they were recovered. The Vietnamese insisted that there were no Americans still being held captive, and the commission concluded the same. Woodcock told the press that the commission was satisfied with what the Vietnamese had done to date and recommended that the U.S. vigorously pursue the normalization of relations.

The National League of POW-MIA Families was extremely disappointed that the Woodcock Commission was satisfied that the Vietnamese had accounted for and returned the remains of only 41 MIA's in four years. The League resented the fact that Carter was attempting to normalize relations with Vietnam before getting a full accounting first. To the families, any compromise was seen as proof that the government was abandoning the MIA's. Congress strongly advocated that the U.S. was not obligated to normalize relations with Vietnam since the "communist takeover" (Vietnam's reunification in 1975) was regarded as a direct violation of the Paris Accords. Congressional opposition prevented Carter from normalizing relations with the SRV during his presidency and, as a result, the Vietnamese continued to sporadically account for MIA's. From 1976 to 1980, only 50 MIA's were accounted for.

The Reagan Administration's Policy

The Reagan Administration's policy has been to isolate Vietnam politically and economically. According to one news magazine, the U.S. effort to "squeeze Vietnam economically" and to keep Vietnam an "international outcast" has reduced Vietnam's economy to the worst shape it has ever been in.

The Reagan Administration's interest in the POW-MIA issue has been growing. Shortly after his election, Reagan declared the MIA's to be an issue of highest national priority, and in May, 1981, the Administration admitted that it had sent two covert patrols into Laos, under the supervision of the CIA, in response to "tantalizing hints" that POW's were still alive there.

While for eight years the Pentagon had adamantly denied that any POW's were still captive, under the current Administration, the Defense Department's attitude has changed strikingly. In June, 1981, Lt. Gen. Eurge Tighe, the retired director of the Defense Intelligence Agency (DIA), told the House Subcommittee on Asian and Pacific Affairs: "My personal conviction and stated assurance is that there is at least one American being held against his will in Indochina. . . . I would suggest that those reports that we take most seriously, of course, involve more than one." In January, 1982, the DIA released a paper which revealed the Pentagon's position that "the conviction that the many reports, the known perfidiousness of the Communist governments in Southeast Asia, the logic that implies some of the many missing must have survived, all suggest that Americans may be alive in Communist controlled Southeast Asia."

The National League of Families, so accustomed to hearing the usual policy line, was astounded by the government's turnaround. Not coincidentally, the League, for so long regarded as a Washington "outcast," is now being courted again by the U.S. government. For the first time in nearly a decade, the MIA families were flown to their 1982 annual convention in military transport. In an unprecedented move, the Reagan Administration symbolically allowed the League's black-and-white POW-MIA flag—bearing the words, "You are not forgotten," under the silhouette of a POW—to fly beneath the American flag at the White House and the Pentagon on July 9, 1982, National POW-MIA Recognition Day. On Jan. 28, 1983—10 years and one day after the Paris Peace Accords were signed—the President told an emotional audience of POW and MIA families that their "vigil" was over.

Whether the President intends to step up diplomatic negotiations, covert activities, or strong-arm politics to pressure the Vietnamese and Laotian governments to resolve the issue is still unclear, but the League is basking in the glow of Reagan's preferential treatment and is elated over the President's concern, which has resulted in heightened media attention and public curiosity. Encouraged, the POW and MIA families are hopeful that the issues will be resolved. Whether or not their "vigil" will soon be over still remains to be seen.

Depending on the political climate, the government's response to the POW-MIA problem has vacillated. When the problem was considered useful to an administration's policies, the government displayed great concern for the POW's and their families. However, when the problem was determined to be disadvantageous to policy, the issue was ignored and repressed. The government chose to create the issue not only to raise the country's patriotic consciousness, but to convince a skeptical American public that the war was necessary as long as the Vietnamese held any American prisoners. Knowing that the captured American pilots were basically the only bargaining chips the North Vietnamese had, the Johnson and Nixon Administrations strategically sanctioned U.S. policy to hinge upon the release of the prisoners. It was not unusual that the enemy was holding prisoners of war, but the U.S. government's use of those prisoners to justify continued involvement in Indochina is an unparalleled event in the history of American warfare.

The POW and MIA families have had a stormy relationship with the U.S. government. The Nixon Administration threw the POW's into the national limelight, and the National League of POW-MIA Families believed that the POW's and MIA's were important to the government. Yet, if the POW's were so important, why did Nixon immediately suppress the issue and the families as soon as the Paris Accords were signed, even though a majority of prisoners and missing did not return from Southeast Asia? Why was the Pentagon more concerned about alleviating its paperwork than with justly determining the status of its missing men? Why didn't the Nixon Administration or Congress make any effort to amend the 1942 Missing Persons Act to realistically apply to the Vietnamese conflict? Why did Gerald Ford refuse a full accounting of the MIA's during the Paris Talks when the Vietnamese were willing to compromise their basic position of insisting for war reparation?

Now, after the government has adamantly insisted for a decade the all American prisoners were dead in Southeast Asia, Reagan had suddenly reversed that policy and has sparked renewed media interest in the problem. What purpose does he have in digging up the issue again after three prior administrations worked so hard to bury it? Is Reagan really interested in resolving the issue, or is he more interested in using the POW-MIA issue to feed the flame of anti-communist rhetoric?

The National League of Families believes that the government is finally listening to their cries. For nearly 14 years, the League has vowed to never let the government forget about the POW's and MIA's, and the families pride themselves at becoming a thorn in the government's side. If the POW and MIA families have been victims of government manipulation, they have certainly been willing victims. It is remarkable that, despite years of being exploited, deserted, and betrayed, the League families have still retained their faith in the American government. Somehow, they still believe that the government will someday resolve the issue simply because their loved ones deserve to be accounted for. This seeming naivete is ironic. In essence, the U.S. government has manipulated its most loyal subjects.

So, the ordeal continues. For the families of the POW's and MIA's, the Vietnam War may never end.

THE MYTH OF THE LOST POWs[6]

Ten years after America's withdrawal from Vietnam, President Reagan has made the recovery of 2,477 American soldiers "the highest national priority." In June 1983 a division of the Defense Intelligence Agency was assigned a large full-time staff to collect and evaluate information about POWs and MIA. Last summer Reagan signed a proclamation designating the third Friday in July as the annual National POW/MIA Recognition Day. A Congressional Task Force on POW/MIAs in Southeast Asia was created in 1977, and in the last several years Congress has introduced more than 100 bills and resolutions aimed at resolving the problem. A number of celebrities, including William Shatner, Gloria Vanderbilt, and Willie Mays, have been promoting public awareness of the issue in books, movies, and fund-raising drives. John LeBoutillier, a former representative from New York, is working with Charlton Heston in a national phone solicitation

[6]Reprint of an article by James Rosenthal, a free-lance writer. New Republic. 193:15, 17–19. Jl. 1, '85. Copyright © 1985 by the New Republic. Reprinted by permission.

campaign to drum up money to help the "American POWs kept in bamboo cages, in the jungle, or in caves in the mountains." As a government official recently told *The New York Times,* "Somehow the mystery of their disappearance and their deaths have taken on a peculiar life of their own."

The popular usage of the term "MIA" is misleading, since it suggests that we have no idea what happened to the soldiers in Vietnam. We do. At the end of the war, the Pentagon listed fewer than 800 soldiers as either prisoners or missing in action. After the war, the Pentagon added to the list servicemen considered killed in action but whose bodies were never recovered. Many of these were Air Force pilots: 81 percent of those now classified as MIAs were pilots, many of whom failed to eject from their planes before crashing in the Vietnamese jungle. (Since 1975 the Vietnamese have returned the remains of about 100 MIAs.)

In fact, of the 2,477 men categorized as MIA, nearly half (1,186) are known to have been killed in action, but their bodies were not recovered. Of those, 436 were Air Force pilots shot down over the sea, whom the Pentagon lists as "non-recoverable." In 647 other cases a presumptive finding of death was made at the time of disappearance. Thus 1,833 of the 2,477 MIAs are known or presumed to be dead. That leaves 644 men who theoretically could still be alive and in Vietnam.

The POW/MIA lobby exploits this uncertainty for all it's worth. In a 1984 *New York Times* Op-Ed piece called "Rotting in Laos," LeBoutillier stated that he has "private sources" who confirm that Americans are still held in Indochina. The organizations of POW/MIA families keep LeBoutillier at arm's length. They make the more modest argument that until there is definitive evidence that the MIAs aren't alive, the U.S. government should act as if they are.

Emotional appeals aside, there is little credible evidence that any of them are still living. Of the 3,508 reports from Indochinese refugees about alleged sightings of missing Americans since 1975, the Defense Intelligence Agency discounts all but five. Only 751 of these alleged sightings were firsthand accounts from Indochinese refugees who claim to have seen—not just heard about—captive Americans. In congressional testimony last August, the director of the DIA, Lieutenant General James Williams, stressed the ambiguity of even these reports. "A lot of these people who talk about live sighting say they have seen an individual who was a Caucasian who they think was an American . . . [and] who looked like he was under guard." According to the DIA, 77 percent of these firsthand reports have been resolved, either by correlating the sighting to men who have since been accounted for, or by determining that the sightings were fabricated.

The DIA has used polygraph exams in investigating the most credible reported sightings. Of approximately 40 witnesses tested since 1979, it says that 24 showed signs of deception, two were inconclusive, and 13 showed no deception. Of those 13, four were of people who have been accounted for, three were sightings of non-prisoners, and one was a fabrication. The remaining five reports represent the best—but by no means conclusive—evidence that Americans are still held in Vietnam.

Other pieces of "evidence" that there are still POWs in Vietnam seem dubious. For example, former U.S. major general John K. Singlaub claims that 13 French POWs captured by the Vietnamese during the siege of Dien Bien Phu in 1954 were not released until 16 years later. A French Embassy spokesman says that all French POWs were released in 1954 and that Singlaub's contention is nonsense.

Some have cited the rambling of Private Robert Garwood as additional evidence that there are still POWs in Vietnam. Garwood was a Marine captured in the 1960s who won the trust of the North Vietnamese and was allowed a measure of freedom. When he returned to the United States in 1979, he was found not guilty of desertion but was court-martialed for collaboration. He told *The Wall Street Journal* last December that he had seen about 70 American POWs while living in Vietnam. Yet when Garwood first returned he only told the DIA of "rumors" of American POWs. His biography, *Conversations with the Enemy: The Story of PFC Robert Garwood,* published in 1983, never mentions POWs. And his own psychiatrist questions the legitimacy of his disclosures, saying that Garwood suffers from many psychological traumas. Even the POW/MIA organizations doubt Garwood's credibility.

The POW/MIA issue is unique to the Vietnam War. After World War II, 78,751 American soldiers were missing or unaccounted for. Their number exceeds by 20,000 the total number of American servicemen *killed* in Vietnam. The Korean War resulted in 8,177 MIAs. Yet neither prompted widespread protests and demands for government inquiries. In part, of course, the reaction to the Vietnam MIAs is because we lost the war. The U.S. has no access to places where missing soldiers were last seen alive, and MIA families felt that the country, in its desire to quickly forget the war, was also forgetting their sons, husbands, and brothers. What's more, the MIAs have become a matter of American honor, and their return a symbolic restoration of that honor. The POW movies, especially Sylvester Stallone's current box-office smash, *Rambo: First Blood Part II,* appeal to these sentiments.

But there is another explanation. Far from forgetting these sons and brothers, the government has put them to undisguised political use. Successive administrations have alternated between actively suppressing the families' requests for information and assisting them in publicizing their cause. The results have been disappointing diplomatically, and cruelly misleading for the families.

In 1966 President Johnson was conducting secret negotiations on the POWs with North Vietnamese officials in Paris. The administration believed it would be detrimental to the talks, as well as to the prisoners, to publicize the problem. Administration officials told the families of POWs and MIAs to keep quiet. Valerie Kushner, an MIA wife, told *Life* magazine in 1970, "I wanted to yell from the first day, but I was told by the Army that they would not only not help me, but squelch me."

Three years later President Nixon, aware of the families' growing frustration, decided to champion their cause through a major policy change. Defense Secretary Melvin Laird announced on May 18, 1969, that the administration would "go public" with the POW issue in an effort to use public opinion to pressure the Vietcong into obeying the Geneva principles concerning POW rights. The campaign was waged through press conferences, speaking engagements by former POWs, and demonstrations by POW and MIA families.

In December 1969 Nixon met with 26 POW wives to suggest
the formation of a national organization of MIA and POW families. From this core, other MIA families were enlisted to march
in Washington on May 1, 1970, in support of the war. On May
28, 1970, hundreds were flown to the capital in military transport
aircraft for the first official meeting of the National League of
Families of Americans Missing in Southeast Asia. Spiro Agnew
presented the League with a check for $10,000 in proceeds from
the sale of Agnew watches and T-shirts. A week later a special
White House telephone WATS line, linking the League to the
White House, was installed in the League's office. Robert P.
Odell, the financial director for the Republican National Committee, planned for the League to use the committee's mailing lists
to raise money for League travel, advertising, and publicity ex-
penses. Joan M. Vinson, then the national coordinator of the
RNC, had written the League's board members that "most importantly, no one will know that we are using the lists owned by the
Republican National Committee." But the arrangement began to
come undone when Representative Les Aspin had the details
printed in *The Congressional Record*. Within the year, the families started questioning the Nixon administration's motives.

By mid-1971, two years after President Nixon had begun his
plan   to   end   U.S.   involvement   in   the   war   through
"Vietnamization," MIA families began to worry. They feared that
the reductions of U.S. troops would mean a reduced commitment
to the POWs and MIAs. This fear was heightened when the families realized that the Nixon administration's plans did not include
any provisions for obtaining the release of POWs or accounting
for MIAs. In anger, 400 families split from the League to form
the antiwar Families for Immediate Release.

Following the Paris Peace Accords of January 1973, which officially ended U.S. involvement in the war, 591 POWs were released from Vietnam. The Hanoi government said that these were
the only prisoners they held. But this only exacerbated the alarm
of the families whose boys did not return. The government, abiding by the Missing Persons Act of 1942, would begin conducting
automatic status reviews on missing servicemen after a year. If

there was no evidence to the contrary, the soldier would be declared KIA (killed in action) and the case closed.

Five people the National League of Families brough suit in a U.S. District Court to stop the Pentagon from changing their relatives' status from MIA to KIA, demanding that the military prove the subjects dead. In August 1973 the court ruled that reviews could be conducted only on the written request of a dependent next of kin. Ironically, the litigation heightened the anxiety of those families who wanted to end the drawn-out trauma. One MIA wife wrote in a letter to the military Status Review Board: "I wish a status review would be held on my husband, however, I will not request one at this time. . . . I would be asking that he be declared dead—something I feel would have psychological implications for my children and my husband's parents. Furthermore, I resent being put in that position by the Military Services—it is their job to determine, on their knowledge, the status of my husband."

For some of the families, no doubt, initally there was a clear financial incentive not to request a review. Benefits to an MIA family at the time were far greater than those awarded to a KIA family. In August 1976 the House Select Committee on MIAs compared the hypothetical case of an air Force captain, with a wife and three children, declared KIA in 1966, with the same individual listed as MIA until a presumptive finding of death was made in 1975. The total benefits paid over the same period to the MIA wife exceeded those paid to the KIA wife by almost $100,000.

But the financial incentive no longer exists. In 1978 the Pentagon declared all MIAs "presumed dead," except for Air Force Colonel Charles E. Shelton, who remains listed as POW for symbolic purposes. A status reclassification change from MIA to Killed in Action/Body Not Recovered routinely results in a sizable lump-sum payment—in the range of $60,000 to $100,000 in addition to substantial child support payments and educational benefits for dependent children.

The plight of the MIA families was complicated by the demands of Hanoi officials. Article 21 of the Paris Peace Accords stipulated that the U.S. "contribute to healing the wounds of war and to post-war construction" in Vietnam. In 1973 President Nixon sent a letter to President Pham Van Dong promising Vietnam $3.25 billion in U.S. economic aid over a five-year period "without political conditions." But Congress refused to grant the aid request. Vietnamese negotiators, feeling betrayed, announced that they wouldn't discuss the MIA issue until the aid came through. At the same time they denied that they held any POWs or knew anything about the fate of other MIAs. The United States insisted that the Vietnamese account for the American MIAs as a prerequisite for resuming diplomatic relations. The deadlock continues to this day.

In the mid-1970s, Congress took up the issue. The House Select Committee on Missing Persons in Southeast Asia concluded investigation of the POW/MIA issue for 15 months. It heard testimony from 50 high-ranking officials (including President Ford, Secretary of State Henry Kissinger, and Secretary of Defense Donald Rumsfeld), held more than 20 executive sessions to discuss classified information, reviewed the files of over 200 soldiers classified as MIA, and petitioned the Pentagon for details on more than 100 of its relevant files. The Select Committee concluded in December 1976 that "no Americans are still being held alive as prisoners in Indochina, or elsewhere, as a result of the war in Indochina."

President Carter, accepting the committee's findings, believed that the next step was to secure the return of any MIA corpses from Vietnamese authorities. He appointed a commission on MIAs headed by the former president of the United Auto Workers union Leonard Woodcock. The Woodcock Commission visited Hanoi in March 1977 under severe handicaps: the group wasn't permitted outside Hanoi, and was forbidden from talking to civilians about the issue. Nevertheless, it agreed with the House Select Committee that there were no American POWs being held in Indochina, and said that the Vietnamese government was doing all it could to account for the MIAs. When in September 1978 Hanoi mysteriously announced its willingness to separate the issues of aid and normalization, it appeared that a substantial accounting of the MIAs was imminent. But President Carter then granted

"official" recognition to China—Vietnam's traditional enemy—
and Vietnam invaded Cambodia. These developments cooled the
slight warming in relations between Washington and Hanoi.

Ironically, Carter's intention to deal directly with Hanoi in an
attempt to confront those capable of returning the dead MIAs only
managed to alienate those he wished to help most: the families.
The National League of Families unanimously rejected the
Woodcock Commission's findings and denounced Carter for
"disposing of the POWs and MIAs" for the sake of resuming relations with Vietnam.

Then came the placebo politics of President Reagan. Without
any new evidence that there might actually be Americans still
alive in Vietnam, Reagan revived the POW/MIA issue. In 1982,
for the first time in nearly a decade, over 450 MIA family members throughout America were flown to their 1982 annual convention in military transport at public expense. There have since been
four other airlifts to Washington, and over 600 MIA family members are expected for this year's convention on July 19. For the
last four years on National POW/MIA Recognition Day, the
League's black-and-white POW/MIA flag—bearing the words
"You Are Not Forgotten"—has flown beneath the American flag
at the White House, the Capitol, and the Pentagon. Reagan has
brought the families to the White House for well-publicized
luncheons and called their cause a "highest national priority." The
way our system works," a White House aide told *The New York
Times,* "if the President is personally interested in something, then
the Government is interested in it. And Mr. and Mrs. Reagan are
personally very interested in MIAs."

These gestures provide no real hope of ending the families'
pain. Reagan has led some of them to believe that they do not have
to accept the loss of their loved ones. During Veterans Day ceremonies last November, he stated that "some [American soldiers]
may still be saved." If, as the president believes, the Vietnamese
have been hiding any POWs all these years, he has hardly given
them an incentive to return them. To recant its previous denials
now would be extremely embarrassing for Hanoi; it might be far
less costly simply to kill the POWs. And for many families the

calls for greater government action have reawakened horrible images of ongoing torture and abuse in some distant jungle.

Over the past decade intelligence information has shown overwhelmingly that the existence of living American MIAs and POWs in Indochina is highly improbable. Why is the issue kept alive? "This issue has been used many ways throughout its history," says Ann Mills Griffiths, executive director of the National League of Families. "It's been used both to justify foreign policy positions and it's been used as a scapegoat for failed policies as well." These families have had their hopes raised by politicians, publishers, filmmakers, and lawyers in pursuit of self-promotion and profits. Of course, every effort should be made to account for and recover the remains of Americans killed in Vietnam. But that is far different from sustaining the cruel delusion that there may be Americans alive in Vietnam.

IV. TEN YEARS LATER: RETROSPECTIVE VIEWS OF THE VIETNAM WAR

EDITOR'S INTRODUCTION

The tenth anniversary of the end of the war in Vietnam has evoked many new books, magazine articles, and television programs. All of the major networks, for example, gave extensive coverage to the anniversary of the end of the war; and two years earlier the Public Broadcasting System ran an ambitious thirteen-part series called *Vietnam: A Television History,* which cost nearly five million dollars and took six years to produce. Yet the issues concerning our involvement in Vietnam are still far from being clarified. Section IV of this volume focuses upon differences of viewpoint about Vietnam.

A first article, reprinted from *Commentary* and written by Norman Podhoretz, the magazine's editor, speaks for the conservative position. Podhoretz maintains, first, that distortions of various kinds appear in the documentary, and, secondly, that its apportioning of blame equally to those who supported the war and those who opposed it lends itself to an attitude of pacifism, a willingness to accept the expansion of Soviet power. The second article, by Hendrik Hertzberg, reprinted from the *New Republic,* attacks the domino theory of American strategists, which has not been borne out by events following the war. He concludes that it was immoral to prosecute a war, bringing incalculable suffering and death, when it could not be won. Then James Chace, in a symposium article from *Harper's,* moderates a discussion of the consequences of Vietnam in current foreign policy debate. The final article, by Secretary of State George P. Shultz, states the position of the administration, arguing that a period of self-doubt following the war coincided with the expansion of Soviet power in such countries as Angola and Afghanistan. The lesson of Vietnam, he concludes, is that the U. S. must be resolute in defense of democracy throughout the world, relying on a variety of options.

VIETNAM: THE REVISED STANDARD VERSION[1]

. . . In spite of these ingenious efforts of denial, however, little by little the onslaught of evidence and sober argument began undermining the idea that the United States and its South Vietnamese allies were the villains of the war while the Vietcong and the North Vietnamese Communists were the heroes. Holding on to Vietnam as a symbol of American malevolence and Communist virtue was therefore becoming increasingly difficult. For those whose intellectual and emotional investment in the antiwar movement's version of Vietnam was so great that giving it up would be tantamount to declaring political bankruptcy, a new defensive line needed to be drawn. That line has now been drawn by Stanley Karnow's book and reinforced by the PBS series entitled *Vietnam: A Television History,* of which Karnow himself was one of the originators," on which he served as "chief correspondent," and to which his book is described as a "companion."

As it happens, there are a number of differences between the book and the television series. Indeed, having been led to believe from a massive and lavishly produced press kit that the series was a straightforward translation by Karnow of the book into a television documentary—with the relation between the two resembling, say, that of Kenneth Clark's book *Civilisation* to the TV series of the same name—I was amazed to find that Karnow neither wrote any of the scripts nor acted as narrator and guide nor even ever appeared on camera.

Be that as it may, both the book and the series have been very widely praised as objective, fair-minded, and well-balanced, and while neither deserves these accolades, the series deserves them a good deal less than the book. For unlike Karnow, the people who wrote and produced several of the thirteen episodes are still trying

[1]Excerpted from an article by Norman Podhoretz, editor of *Commentary*. *Commentary*. 77: 37–41. Ap. '84. Copyright © 1984 by *Commentary*. Reprinted by permission.

to push the old version of the story, with the Communists cast in the role of heroes and the Americans and the South Vietnamese represented as villains.

This becomes immediately clear in the first two episodes which mainly deal with the Vietnamese struggle for independence against the French. These episodes are made up in large part of interviews and film footage taken from North Vietnam and taken, moreover, almost entirely at face value. The predictable result is a portrait of Ho Chi Minh as an almost saintly figure; his lieutenants, too—men like Pham Van Dong and General Vo Nguyen Giap, whose policies have brought nothing but war, destitution, and the terrors of totalitarianism to the people of Vietnam—are consistently presented in flattering poses and allowed self-serving interviews.

In general, the impression conveyed is that the Vietnamese Communists were and are people of courage, integrity, singleness of purpose, and selfless love of country. The South Vietnamese, by equally predictable contrast, are for the most part shown throughout the series as corrupt, unprincipled, incompetent, cruel, and selfish. We repeatedly hear them denounced as "puppets" by Pham Van Dong and other Communist leaders, and the way they are portrayed—wholly dependent on the United States and unable or unwilling to fight for themselves—lends tacit credence to this characterization. At the same time, the South Vietnamese are repeatedly being denounced on the screen by Americans who complain that they refused to institute various reforms urged upon them by Washington. Yet it never seems to occur to the authors of the series that the stubbornness of South Vietnam's leaders—first Ngo Dinh Diem and then Nguyen Van Thieu—makes nonsense of the charge that they were American puppets.

In several episodes, the attitude of the series toward the United States also bears traces of the anti-Americanism that was so prominent and so ugly a feature of the antiwar movement. The CIA is accused of responsibility for the flight of a million refugees from North to South after the Geneva Accords dividing the country had been signed in 1954 (when in fact most of these refugees were Catholics who needed no encouragement from the CIA or anyone else to flee from Communist rule); Lyndon Johnson is accused of caring more about domestic politics than about containing Communism (when in fact he sacrificed his Presidency to his belief in containment); American soldiers are shown weeping over what we are led to believe were atrocities (when in fact the responsibility, both moral and legal, for battlefield tactics that caused civilian casualties rested with an enemy who fought by hiding behind civilians); and the influence of Shawcross is all over the episode on the war in Cambodia.

Insidious editing tricks, amounting to outright lies, are also used to reinforce the anti-American appeal. "We're trying to do the reasonable thing," says the voice of Lyndon Johnson as images flash by of Marines blowing up a village, of mangled corpses, and of weeping children. (The lie here is that it was the Americans rather than the North Vietnamese who stood in the way of a negotiated settlement, when in truth the North Vietnamese, as they themselves now freely admit, never had any interest in compromise and were single-mindedly pursuing victory.) Or again: an American veteran of the war, talking about his experience, is shown saying that trying to kill someone "sends a real charge through you," and an American soldier is pictured wearing a helmet with the inscription "Kill a gook for God," while a chaplain leads a company in the field in the singing of "Onward Christian Soldiers." (Here the lie is that the American troops in Vietnam were bloodthirsty and mindlessly self-righteous, when in truth— as other episodes indicate—most of them had an ironic sense of themselves as "the unwilling, led by the unqualified, doing the unnecessary for the ungrateful," which is what the much more characteristic helmet inscription "UUUU" stood for.) Or again: the Christmas 1972 bombing of Hanoi is mainly represented by footage of a hospital that had been hit, with the camera dwelling almost lovingly on wounded children and outraged doctors. (The lie here is the suggestion that the bombing was indiscriminate, when in truth American pilots were threatened with court-martial if they deviated from prescribed bombing runs designed to minimize civilian casualties, with the result that such casualties were indeed kept to a minimum.)

In the eyes of this series, the only good thing about the United States was the antiwar movement. But the antiwar movement we acutally see on the screen and hear about from the invisible narrator is as sanitized and idealized as the North Vietnamese. Though we get a glimpse of Jerry Rubin and another of Stokely Carmichael, in only one quick shot—a sign with a swastika carried by a protester—are we given any real indication that the movement consistently vilified the United States and the South Vietnamese, while either supporting the Vietcong and the North Vietnamese or lying about their character and purposes. The antiwar movement we see here seems to be made up entirely of sober dissenters like George Ball and Mike Mansfield, anguished veterans whose eyes had been opened by the horrors of the war, and earnest young idealists being clubbed by the cops.

As Stephen J. Morris points out in a piece in the *Wall Street Journal*, however, most of this kind of thing is confined to the episodes which were done either by French-or-British producers. Those episodes that were produced by an American team under Richard Ellison at WGBH in Boston are in general neither pro-Communist nor anti-American. Moreover, because even the French- and British-made episodes were toned down as a result of criticism from outside academic consultants, the impression left by the series as a whole, and explicitly conveyed by the concluding episode (written and produced by Ellison himself), is more even-handed than some of the individual pieces. In that sense, it can be said that the series is a "companion" to Karnow's book, even though the book is on many points of detail as well as in its overall perspective better balanced and far more honest.

Thus, writing as a critic of American policy, Karnow nevertheless tries to go where the evidence leads even when it undermines the antiwar case. While recognizing, for example, that three times as many bombs were dropped on North Vietnam as the United States used in all of World War II, he also takes care to emphasize that these bombs did far less damage because they were directed only at military targets:

The dikes along the Red River, whose destruction would have flooded the valley and killed hundreds of thousands of people, were never targeted.

Nor were North Vietnam's cities subjected to the kind of "carpet bombing" that obliterated Dresden and Tokyo [in World War II]. Bombs devastated parts of North Vietnam, particularly the area above the seventeenth parallel where troops and supplies were massed to move south, but Hanoi and Haiphong were hardly bruised.

Unlike the TV series, Karnow also gives a reasonably balanced account of the Christmas 1972 bombing. He mentions the "ghastly results" of bombs that went astray, such as the one that accidentally hit the hospital which is featured on the TV series. But he does not dwell disproportionately on these results, because he recognizes that the figures of civilian casualties (about 1,600 for both Hanoi and Haiphong) dispose of the charges of carpet or terror bombing: he knows that the reason these figures were so low was that "the B-52s were programmed to spare civilians, and they pinpointed their targets with extraordinary precision"; and he also recognizes that the North Vietnamese, so often represented as helpless, were well-enough equipped with surface-to-air missiles to shoot down 26 U.S. aircraft, among them 15 B-52's. (What he fails to say is that these losses would have been lighter if the pilots had not been forbidden to deviate from their prescribed flight plans even to avoid being hit.)

If Karnow is not disposed to put the Americans in the worst possible light, or to lend easy credence to the anti-American lies of the old antiwar movement, neither is he inclined to whitewash the North Vietnamese and the Vietcong. One major example, to which I have already alluded, is his acknowledgment that North Vietnamese regulars were sent to the South not in response to American escalation, as has so often been claimed, but "months before the U.S. Marines splashed ashore at Danang in March 1965," and also before the bombing of the North began.

In addition, he confirms the contention earlier advanced by Lewy and the French journalist Jean Lacouture (though without citing them) that the Vietcong was an instrument of the North Vietnamese, thus dispelling what he himself calls "the myth, in which many Westerners then believed, that the Vietcong was essentially an indigenous and autonomous insurgent movement." And in his section on the Tet offensive, he minces no words about the atrocities the Communists committed in Hue where they "displayed unprecedented brutality, slaughtering minor government functionaries and other innocuous figures as well as harmless foreign doctors, schoolteachers, and missionaries."

Nor, finally, does he make any bones about the results of the Communist victory in Vietnam. He speaks of the "Vietnamese gulag" created by the Communists, of the destitution resulting from their management of the economy, of the boat people, and of the transformation of the country into a Soviet dependency.

All this no doubt helps to account for the enthusiasm with which such hawkish reviewers as Harry G. Summers and Douglas Pike have greeted Karnow's book. But I would guess that the book owes its success in dovish circles to something else—to the general interpretation it offers of what happened in Vietnam and why.

This interpretation (which the TV series echoes) might be summarized as follows: The Vietnamese nationalist movement, led by Ho Chi Minh, was determined at all costs to achieve independence. After driving the French out, Ho Chi Minh was forced to accept a temporary division of his country and he then went to war through his surrogates the Vietcong to unify the nation under his rule. The United States, mistakenly seeing Ho as an instrument of international Communism, intervened, making the further mistake of believing that the increasing application of American power would persuade him to give up his goal. During the course of the war, many stupid and vicious things were done by both sides, and both countries, each in its own way, suffered considerable damage. In the end, Hanoi's determination proved greater than Washington's and the Americans, like the French before them, were driven out, opening the way at last for the unification of Vietnam under an indigenous nationalist regime. Ironically, however, victory was no kinder to Vietnam than defeat was to the United States. Vietnam was now unified and independent, but the people were repressed and impoverished. This, then, was "The War Nobody Won."

In developing this version of the story (which, incidentally, represents a return to the main lines of the standard version accepted during the war itself by liberal critics like David Halberstam), Karnow does not deny that Ho Chi Minh and his followers were Communists as well as nationalists. Yet he seems incapable of taking this fact seriously. At one point, he goes so far as to say that if not for "French intransigence [which] steered him toward violence," Ho might have become, "like Gandhi, an apostle of passive resistance"—this, of one of the more ruthless Leninists of our time. In a similar vein, Karnow repeatedly deplores the "antiquated Marxist ideology" that led the Vietnamese Communists to commit "blunders" and "errors" that a more "realistic" assessment of their own interests would have permitted them to avoid. In other words, Karnow cannot get it through his head that what Ho Chi Minh wanted, and what his followers have achieved, was not merely an independent Vietnam: it was a *Communist* Vietnam. Therefore it is absurd to say that nobody won the Vietnam war. The Communists won; and the hideous results—give or take a local variation or two—were similar to the results of Communist victories in all the other countries whose people have been cursed with such victories.

But what of the United States? The implication of Karnow's version of the story is that if only the United States had supported Ho Chi Minh instead of opposing him, all would have been well. As a nationalist, he would have been happy to lessen his dependence on the Soviet Union and China, and the fact that he was also a Communist need no more have stood in the way of American support for him than it had in the case of Tito (or than it later would in the case of Mao Zedong).

Just as Karnow fails to take Communism seriously as a factor in Ho Chi Minh's behavior, then, so he fails to take anti-Communism seriously as a factor in the foreign policy of the United States. For it was never merely Russian imperialism that the United States was trying to "contain" through the Marshall Plan, NATO, the Korean War, and then the Vietnam war. It was also the system of Communist totalitarianism that went along with the expansion of Soviet power and influence. To support Yugoslavia, a Communist country breaking away from Soviet domination, was one thing; but it would have been quite another to support a Communist faction fighting against non-Communist and anti-Communist rivals for control of a country which had not yet been drawn into the Soviet orbit.

Though there were a few people in the State Department and elsewhere who favored trying to coopt Ho Chi Minh (and Mao Zedong as well), the consensus in the United States—and it was a bipartisan consensus in which liberal Democrats were even more enthusiastic participants than conservative Republicans— rejected any such policy. Karnow himself quotes Dean Acheson, Harry Truman's Secretary of State, who once dismissed as "irrelevant" the question of whether Ho was "as much nationalist as Commie" because "all Stalinists in colonial areas are nationalists." On another occasion (not cited by Karnow), Acheson told the British Prime Minister Clement Attlee, who had suggested that a more sympathetic policy toward Communist China might encourage Mao to move in a Titoist direction, that the American people could not be expected to support an "interventionist" (i.e., anti-Communist) policy in Europe and an "isolationist" one in the Far East. Acheson's Republican successor, John Foster Dulles (though his behavior in office was much less bellicose than Acheson's and certainly more restrained than his own rhetoric), also regarded Ho Chi Minh as "an arm of Communist aggression." And so too did his Democratic successor Dean Rusk, not to mention the four Presidents of both parties (Truman, Eisenhower, Kennedy, and Johnson) for whom these men all worked.

The point is that it is unhistorical to argue for an alternative policy in the past that had no chance of being adopted. Nor do subsequent events prove, as is so often suggested, that the Americans were wrong about "international Communism." For China *was* subservient to the Soviet Union at least until the end of the 50's and Ho Chi Minh remained so to the end; moreover, "wars of national liberation" *were* encouraged and supported by the Chinese and the Soviets as a prudent way of expanding Communist power and influence in Third World countries like Vietnam. Those who ridicule the idea that there was a monolithic Communist movement directed from Moscow in this period are either being dishonest or do not know what they are talking about. Nor is it at all clear that the subsequent break between the Soviet Union and China, or between China and Vietnam, could have been hastened or manipulated by a different American policy.

Yet if Karnow's book, and still more the TV series, are unhistorical in dealing with the spirit of the past, they are both exquisitely attuned to the spirit of the present. To interpret Vietnam as "The War Nobody Won" plays with perfect harmony into the pacifist attitudes that have become so widespread in the past few years; and so does all the gory combat footage running through the TV series. Not long ago the purpose of dwelling on such images would have been to expose the evils of the American intervention, and while (to repeat) some of that remains in some episodes, the main purpose now is to stress, in true pacifist style, the horrors of war itself.

Similarly, to interpret the American intervention as a mistake rather than as a crime is nicely consonant with an atmosphere in which patriotic feeling has been crowding out the anti-Americanism of the old antiwar movement. Finally, to locate this mistake in the American failure to understand that nationalism is a more powerful force than Communism fits perfectly with the increasingly fashionable idea that the United States should be supporting the guerrillas in El Salvador and the Sandinistas in Nicaragua as nationalists instead of opposing them as Communists linked with the Soviet Union through Cuba.

In short, at a moment when the old antiwar case has been losing its credibility, Karnow and his television colleagues have produced a kind of Revised Standard Version of the story that salvages Vietnam for the fall-back position, which is that American power ought to be used not to oppose Communism but to coopt it, not to make the world safe for democracy but to make it safe for "Titoism." Thanks to the Revised Standard Version, Vietnam, no longer useful as a symbol of American evil and Communist virtue, will now more and more be taken as a definitive demonstration of the stupidity of anti-Communism, the sanctity and power of nationalism, and the futility of resorting to force. No wonder so many people have moved from merely invoking Vietnam to talking happily about it again.

WHY THE WAR WAS IMMORAL[2]

Was the war in Vietnam wrong? Not just inadvisable, not just a costly mistake, but morally wrong? How one answers that depends partly, I guess, on how one experienced the war and the opposition to it. A few days ago, at the university where I'm spending a semester, I found myself deep in conversation with a tutor in the philosophy department, an intense, articulate man five or six years younger than I am. (I'm 41.) We were talking about our experiences in the antiwar movement—ten and 15 and nearly 20 years ago—and he said that when he looks back on that time he feels mostly a kind of angry regret. He had been a member of Students for a Democratic Society when SDS dropped its homegrown ideology of participatory democracy in favor of mindless Maoism; he had chanted, "Ho! Ho! Ho Chi Minh! NLF is gonna win!": he had longed for the triumph of the forces of "liberation" not only in Vietnam but everywhere in the Third World and ultimately at home; he had spelled it Amerika and dismissed its political system—"bourgeois democracy"—as a hoax, a cover for racism and imperialism. When the war ended and Indochina vanished into blood-soaked totalitarianism (instead of the gentle egalitarianism he had expected), he was wrenchingly disillusioned. Gradually he discovered that the "revolutionary socialism" of the Third World is brutal, that the Soviet Union is armed and dangerous, that for all its flaws American democracy is the moral superior of any form of communism. "I was wrong, just totally wrong," he told me. Last year he voted for Reagan.

I was luckier. I happened to have been brought up in a political and moral atmosphere of left-wing anti-communism. Reared on Orwell, Gandhi, and Silone, it was no great trick for me to avoid the more blatant naïvetés of New Leftism, and thus also to avoid the subsequent disillusionments. I took my antiwar arguments from Theodore Draper, not Noam Chomsky; from *Commentary* (yes, *Commentary*) and *The New Republic,* not the

[2]Reprint of an article by Hendrik Hertzberg, author of articles on political affairs. *New Republic.* 192:13–16. Ap. 29, '85. Copyright © 1985 by the *New Republic.* Reprinted by permission.

National Guardian and *Monthly Review*. I was similarly lucky in my encounter with military service. Opposed to what was then still called the "Vietnam policy," yet not so fiercely opposed as to be willing to risk prison, and too straight to dodge the draft, I signed up at the end of 1966 for a three-year hitch in the Navy. I asked to be sent to Vietnam, figuring a desk job in Saigon would be interesting without being unduly risky, but was sent—catch-22—to a sleepy shore billet in New York instead. Two years later I *was* ordered to Vietnam (desk job in Da Nang); but by then my antiwar convictions had grown so strong I preferred jail to further military service, and I announced my intention to refuse the orders. I hoped for antiwar martyrdom; instead, quite by chance, a medical difficulty developed, and I was hastily mustered out. I'd managed to have it both ways: veteran (sort of), and resister (in a way). In the Navy and after, I campaigned for Bobby Kennedy and Allard Lowenstein and other antiwar politicians; went on all the marches; hung around the office of a lively little pacifist weekly, *Win,* whose editor had two stickers on the bumper of his Volkswagen: US OUT OF VIETNAM and RUSSIA OUT OF LATVIA. But I didn't join any of what the inimitable Norman Podhoretz calls (in *Why We Were in Vietnam*) "the three main currents of the 'antiwar' movement": pro-Communist, anti-anti-Communist, and anti-American. I guess that I (along with more prominent opponents of the war, such as Podhoretz himself) must have joined one of the non-main currents. Perhpas it was the current that cheered when Norman Thomas, whom I had been taught to revere and who never disappointed, advised the movement to wash the flag, not burn it.

It's no surprise that the differences over Vietnam, rooted as they are in such different experiences, persist in the form of different histories remembered, different lessons learned. The war turned my tutor friend into a "communist" and me into a pacifist. A decade later, neither of us is what we were. We are merely a Republican and a Democrat, passing the time in earnest conversation. And I still think the war was immoral. So when my tutor friend told me the story of his days in the movement, I readily agreed with him that he had been wrong. "It could have been worse, though," I added. "You could have *supported* the war."

There were always two main arguments in favor of the war, the geopolitical and the "moral." The war's aftermath has undermined the first argument, but has seemingly strengthened the second. For the aftermath proved to be at once worse than the war's opponents had predicted and better than its supporters had feared—worse for the Indochinese, better for everyone else.

The geopolitical argument took many forms, some of which lay in ruins long before the war ended. The notion that the war was needed to stop Sino-Soviet expansionism, for example, had become an embarrassment well before Nixon arrived in Peking. So had the notion that the war was needed to convince the Chinese to abandon revolution and follow the Soviet example of peaceful coexistence.

The most persistent form of the geopolitical argument was the domino theory. Some of the war's retrospective defenders maintain that the fall of Cambodia and Laos proves that the theory was correct. Not so. Cambodia and Laos were Vietnam battlefields long before the Americans arrived, and by the end the three countries became one domino. Anyway, the domino theory always encompassed more than Indochina. Even in its most modest version it envisaged the loss of all Southeast Asia, which is to say Thailand, Burma, and Malaysia. And in its more grandiose form it predicted that Indonesia, India, Australia, and Hawaii would topple too. None of this has happened; on the contrary, the American position in Asia and the Pacific is stronger now than it was before 1975. Such troubles as do exist there, such as instability in the Philippines, cannot remotely be traced to the defeat in Vietnam.

A milder corollary to the domino theory was the argument from will: we needed to go on fighting in Vietnam in order to demonstrate our resolve and reliability. This argument implicitly recognized that the fate of Vietnam was, by itself, peripheral to the national security of the United States; it shifted the ground of discussion from the geopolitics of the map to the geopolitics of the soul. Yes, their will to rid their country of foreigners was stronger than our will to demonstrate our will; but by any reasonable standard, our resolve was strong. We did far, far more than enough to meet our treaty obligations, demonstrate our will, and prove our reliability. We financed a quarter of a century of war in Vietnam.

We fought there in strength for ten years—longer than we fought in World War II, or in Korea, longer than in all of them put together. Fifty-eight thousand American soldiers were killed. We said we would fight, therefore we must fight: at many a juncture along the way that logic seemed compelling. But it was not a compelling reason to fight forever. Our guarantees were not worthless. It was the war that was worthless.

The importance of the collapse of the domino theory to the debate over the war's morality is that the theory, if correct, could arguably have justified an enormous degree of suffering and death. What if it had really been true that the loss of Vietnam would doom Australia, India, Hawaii, and the rest to war followed by Communist totalitarianism? A firm moral case can be made that preventing the certain devastation and enslavement of many countries can justify the destruction, even the total destruction, of one. "We had to destroy this village in order to save a hundred villages" is a defensible proposition. But "we had to destroy this village in order to save it" is a moral absurdity. When the domino theory fell, so, domino-like, did one of the moral props of the war.

We are left, then, with the "moral case," as Podhoretz calls it—the view that the war was moral because it was an attempt to save South Vietnam from Communism. My tutor friend, back in his SDS days, did not think this a moral aim, would not have thought it a moral aim even if it could have been achieved without cost. In thinking these things he made a moral error, and he is right to rue it. Even those of us who took the view that it did not make much difference to the South Vietnamese whether they lived under Communism or under the Saigon regime made a moral error. Take away the war and the Saigon regime, with all its noisy corruption and repressiveness, was morally preferable to the totalitarian silence that now rules, with scarcely less corruption, in Ho Chi Minh City. Except that you can't take away the war.

The overwhelming majority of those who opposed the war did not in any case reject the aim of saving South Vietnam from Communism. And to the extent that the war was fought for this aim if was fought for a moral aim. But this says no more than that the war was fought with good intentions rather than evil ones, which is saying very little. If good intentions were enough, there would be no neoconservatives.

In war the moral question is always the same: does the end justify the means? The calculations are necessarily ugly, but they are unavoidable. Ten years ago the choice was not between a Communist South Vietnam and a non-Communist one. It was between a Communist South Vietnam on the one hand, and the terrible cost of keeping South Vietnam non-Communist on the other. The aftermath of the war—the boat people, the "reeducation" camps, above all the unimaginable horror that engulfed Cambodia—has made the "moral case," the argument that the war was worth fighting solely for the sake of the people of Indochina, seem much more plausible than it did at the time. But for the "moral case" to be clinched, the war must be judged to have been winnable—winnable, moreover, at a lower cost in suffering and death than the cost of the Communist victory.

The retrospective defenders of the war must argue that the war could have been won, and their arguments mostly take the form of "if only." If only the bombers had hit "worthwhile targets" on their 1,000 sorties a day, says the military analyst Edward Luttwak in a current *Harper's* symposium, it "would have ended the war in a day." If only Lyndon Johnson had rallied the country behind the war as a moral imperative, writes Podhoretz in his Vietnam book, then the American people would have remained steadfast. If only the United States had followed a purposeful military strategy, argues Harry G. Summers in *On Strategy: A Critical Analysis of the Vietnam War*, then the conditions for a successful South Vietnamese war against the Vietcong might have been created. If only Congress hadn't voted down supplementary military aid to the Saigon government in 1975, contends Richard Nixon in his new book, *No More Vietnams*, then everything might have turned out fine.

All of these arguments rest on the assumption that there was a point at which North Vietnam, having calculated that the actual costs of war were exceeding the prospective benefits of victory, would have stopped fighting. It seems clearer than ever today that there was no such point. Some people understood this at the time. Ten years ago, this magazine published a special issue devoted to the end of the war. Richard Holbrooke, who had resigned in protest from the foreign service, and who later became an assistant secretary of state, began his essay with these words:

For at least eight years it seemed reasonable to me to assume that sooner or later, no matter what we did in Vietnam, things would end badly for us. This feeling was not based on any desire to see us humiliated, or any feeling that the other side represented the forces of goodness and light; it just seemed that the only way to stave off an eventual Communist victory was with an open-ended, and therefore endless, application of American firepower in support of the South Vietnamese regime. No matter how much force we were willing to use, this would not end the war, only prevent Saigon's defeat. And the human suffering would be bottomless. The war would go on until the North Vietnamese achieved their objectives.

Holbrooke's judgment has stood up well. "The essential reality of the struggle," wrote Stanley Karnow in *Vietnam: A History,* published in 1983, "was that the Communists, imbued with an almost fanatical sense of dedication to a reunified Vietnam under their control, saw the war against the United States and its South Vietnamese ally as the continuation of two thousand years of resistance to Chinese and later French rule. They were prepared to accept limitless casualties to attain their sacred objective. Ho Chi Minh, their leader, had made that calculation plain to the French as they braced for war in the late 1940s. 'You can kill ten of my men for every one I kill of yours,' he warned them, 'but even at those odds, you will lose and I will win.'" William Broyles Jr., who fought in Vietnam 15 years ago as a Marine officer, and who recently went back for a visit during which he talked to hundreds of his former enemies, has a similar assessment. Writing in the April *Atlantic,* he concludes, "Whatever the price of winning the war—twenty more years of fighting, another million dead, the destruction of Hanoi—the North Vietnamese were willing to pay it."

If the North Vietnamese were willing to accept limitless casualties, if they were willing to pay any price, then the war could not have been won except by the physical destruction of North Vietnam and the killing of a large proportion of its people. A million? Three million? Six million? The shrill accusation of some in the antiwar movement that the war was "genocidal" was not entirely without justice. Of course no American wanted to kill everybody in North Vietnam. Americans are not monsters. But Americans are not losers, either. Americans are winners. But the logic of winning in Vietnam was inescapably the logic of genocide. We did not lose in Vietnam. We chose not to win. If our entry into the war had something to do with preserving our values, so did our exit from it.

Even Podhoretz, in his book on Vietnam, admits repeatedly that the war could not have been won. In the end, he writes, "The United States demonstrated that saving South Vietnam from Communism was not only beyond its reasonable military, political, and intellectual capabilities but that it was ultimately beyond its moral capabilities as well." Yes, it was beyond our moral capabilities—except that what he understands as a moral failure I understand as a moral success. It wasn't cowardice that finally impelled us to quit. It was conscience.

The old arguments for the war still walk among us, zombie-like, in the form of the theory of the Vietnam syndrome, a term calculated to make the American people's desire to avoid another Vietnam sound pathological rather than prudent. Of course, if the war did result in a syndrome, if it did result in a paralysis of American will and so forth, that is hardly an argument that the war was a good idea. Nor do the follies of parts of the antiwar movement somehow vindicate the war. On the contrary, the antiwar movement was created by the war. Is it really so surprising that this unending, unwinnable war became a machine for producing irrationality, hysteria, and rage? The conservatives' anger at the antiwar movement is misplaced.

The actual consequences of this so-called syndrome are highly problematic. We "lost" Iran after Vietnam, but we "lost" Cuba before it. A more precise effect of the war upon the American political psyche was diagnosed in 1971 by Nathan Glazer, who wrote in a famous *Commentary* article titled "Vietnam: The Case for Immediate Withdrawal" that "the experience of Vietnam has turned the American people into haters of war." That seems exactly right. By August 1964, 300 Americans had been killed and 1,000 wounded in Vietnam. Yet there were only half-dozen American correspondents reporting on the war. (Meanwhile President Johnson was running as the peace candidate, with the support of SDS.) Such relative public indifference to a war with

American deaths running into the hundreds would be unthinkable today. It took years for any significant movement of protest to develop against the Vietnam War. The premises of U.S. involvement were scarcely questioned for the first 15 years. But if the Reagan administration launches an invasion of Nicaragua today, thousands of church people are ready to commit civil disobedience tomorrow. And before giving its support to the new war, the public would insist on a full and prompt discussion of its aims, purposes, and prospects—not out of cynicism or morbid suspicion, but out of a healthy, skeptical, democratic spirit of self-government. War can sometimes be a necessity, but is always to be abhorred. Yes, we were right to oppose the Vietnam War, all of us. Even my friend the Reagan-voting ex-SDSer. Even Norman Podhoretz.

WHAT ARE THE CONSEQUENCES OF VIETNAM?[3]

In the ten years since the last Marine was plucked from the roof of the besieged U.S. Embassy in Saigon, "Vietnam" has come to stand for a good deal more than America's first military defeat. The word calls up images of students battling National Guardsmen in tear-gas clouded streets, of journalists harrying politicians with hostile questions, of critics hounding American presidents from office. "Vietnam" stands for America's loss of innocence.

How have Americans endured this loss? Though policymakers and pundits issue grave warnings about "the lessons of Vietnam," the bitter foreign policy disputes of recent years—over Central America, Grenada, Lebanon—suggest that Vietnam has taught no lessons, at least none Americans can agree on. Nonetheless, the war has had consequences—most important, it has called into question America's sacred mission in the world.

How has Vietnam affected the United States' foreign and military policies? How has it changed Americans' image of their country? How has it influenced American politics and society? *Harper's* recently invited a group of historians, a military analyst, a political consultant, an economist, and a novelist to reflect on the consequences of Vietnam.

[3]Reprint of a symposium article by James Chace, an editor of *The New York Times Book Review*, and others. *Harper's*. 270:35–46. Ap. '85. Copyright © 1985. Reprinted by permission.

The following Forum is based on a discussion held at the Harvard Club in New York City. James Chace served as moderator.

JAMES CHACE was for many years managing editor of *Foreign Affairs* and is currently an editor of the *New York Times Book Review*. His books include *Solvency: An Essay on American Foreign Policy* and *Endless War: How We Got Involved in Central America—And What Can Be Done.*

PAUL M. KENNEDY is Dilworth Professor of History at Yale. His books include *Strategy and Diplomacy, 1870–1945* and *The Rise and Fall of British Naval Mastery*. He is at work on *The Dynamics of World Power from 1500 to the Year 2000.*

EDWARD N. LUTTWAK is a senior fellow at Georgetown University's Center for Strategic and International Studies. His most recent book is *The Pentagon and the Art of War: The Question of Military Reform.*

FRANCES FITZGERALD writes frequently for the *New Yorker*, the *New York Review of Books,* and other publications. Her books include *Fire in the Lake: The Vietnamese and the Americans in Vietnam* and *America Revised.*

PETER MARIN is a novelist and essayist who has written on the moral and cultural issues raised by the Vietnam War for the *Nation, Harper's, Psychology Today,* and other publications. He is currently at work on a book entitled *Conscience and the Common Good.*•

KEVIN P. PHILLIPS is president of the American Political Research Corporation and editor of *American Political Report*. His books include *The Emerging Republican Majority, Post-Conservative America,* and, most recently, *Staying on Top: The Business Case for a National Industrial Strategy.*

GEORGE GILDER is author of *Sexual Suicide, Visible Man, Wealth and Poverty,* and, most recently, *The Spirit of Enterprise.*

James Chace: Whether we like it or not, the American experience in Indochina deeply affects the way we live now. Ten years after the last Marine was lifted off the roof of our doomed embassy in Saigon, the traces of that conflict are present everywhere in this country—in our military's attitude toward foreign involvements, in the design of our foreign policy, in the structure of our domestic politics, and, perhaps most evidently, in the conflicting images Americans have of their country's role in the world.

It was only a generation ago, when John F. Kennedy was president and our creeping involvement in Southeast Asia was scarcely noticed, that the United States seemed omnipotent. Then,

Americans were truly the "watchmen on the walls of world freedom," as the young president wrote in the speech he was to deliver in Dallas on the day he was assassinated.

Today, when Americans speak darkly of the "lessons of Vietnam," that confident talk of American omnipotence seems very far away. Most attempts to exert American power abroad in recent years—the tentative intervention in Lebanon, for example, or the entire U.S. policy in Central America—have been beset by controversy. Indeed, Americans seem unable to agree on what the lessons of Vietnam *are,* at least as regards the central question of where and under what circumstances the United States should use military force abroad. While many see in the myth of American omnipotence a dangerous illusion that might again lead us into futile adventures abroad, others want to reconstruct the myth, or, in any event, to restore to America the role of world leader it played before its failure in Vietnam.

Our subject today is not the lessons but the consequences of Vietnam. Our task is to search out the traces Vietnam has left on the America of 1985. Where precisely do we find the consequences of Vietnam in today's America? Have we overcome any of the effects of Vietnam? Is America, in Ronald Reagan's words, "standing tall" again?

I thought we might begin by considering what would seem to be the most direct consequences of the Vietnam War—the military ones. From there we can move on to the larger social and moral questions of how the war has affected American behavior both at home and abroad, and how it is likely to do so in the future. Paul Kennedy, as a military historian, what do you see as the main military consequences of the Vietnam War?

Paul M. Kennedy: Well, it's dificult to separate the specific effects the Vietnam War has had on America's role in the world from the much larger, structural changes that have gradually transformed the international balance of power during the last twenty-five years. Of course, the direct consequences of the war on our military are fairly clear. America now has a noticeably cautious Pentagon, a military establishment that nervously questions itself about when and in what circumstances it can intervene aboard without getting bogged down in an unpopular, divisive war. As is evident from Secretary of Defense Weinberger's speech last November on U.S. military policy, the Pentagon is demanding to know where it can fight and be *assured* of public support; which is to say, our military is submitting its strategy to a sort of "Vietnam litmus test." And the obvious consequences of *that* consequence is that the United States has become a very cautious imperial power.

That much is pretty straightforward. The problems arise when we try to separate the specific military consequences from other important changes that have tended to complicate America's role in the world, but that probably would have occurred in any event, even if the war had never happened. For example, in the last quarter-century or so we have witnessed an enormous change in Third World attitudes toward the United States. Many Third World governments have reacted strongly against what they consider an overwhelming American presence, against the growing influence of American capital and the American culture and mores that have come with it. During the same period our European allies have become stronger and more independent, and less willing to follow America's lead unquestioningly in matters of foreign policy. Finally, and perhaps most important, the Russians succeeded in closing the gap in strategic nuclear forces, and the United States lost its position as the clearly predominant superpower.

These gradual transformations, and others we could name, have combined to give Americans the very definite sense that the world is no longer their oyster. And all of them would have occurred even if Vietnam had never happened.

Edward N. Luttwak: Your analysis implies that the world after Vietnam has achieved a new equilibrium, an equilibrium that includes an inevitably diminished American role. My own assessment is quite different: I believe the war, and its effect on America's willingness to exert its power, has led to world disequilibrium.

Let's look more closely at the purely military consequences of the war. You mentioned the so-called Weinberger doctrine, which basically says that operations like Grenada represent a ceiling on the level of military action the Pentagon is willing to contemplate.

Weinberger essentially declared to the world, "We will apply military force only if we know we're going to win quickly and easily, and only if we are *guaranteed* total support from the public." I think his statement accurately reflects the views of our professional military. I believe this is a wholly praiseworthy doctrine—wonderfully suited to a country such as Switzerland, which promises to come to the aid of no other nation, guarantees no order to the world, and, in short, is content to live in a world in which events are dominated by others. But for a country such as the United States, the Weinberger doctrine is completely and absurdly unsuitable.

What are the consequences of this attitude—the consequences of the consequences of Vietnam? Consider the American performance in El Salvador. The American military, in supervising the war, is imposing its current preoccupation with its great rearmament program, a program that obviously must be sustained politically. The military believes it is very bad business indeed to get involved in Central America: let's not erode the political basis for our new weapons by getting enmeshed in what might become a very unpopular war in El Salvador—that's the Pentagon's attitude.

Hence the President's Central America policy is supported only most reluctantly by the military. It makes no effort to ensure that the pitifully few advisers we have in El Salvador are the very best men; fifty-five people are simply assigned to El Salvador as if it were Germany or Korea. The military makes no attempt to guarantee that the miserable amount of American aid is even applied to acquiring and maintaining suitable weapons. Instead, the military's standard issue weapons, intended for the world's richest armed forces, are given to the world's poorest. This is just lack of professional attention.

My point is that America's military has been thoroughly corrupted. Not in the trivial sense of soldiers stealing or taking bribes—in that sense the American military is uniquely honest. The military has been corrupted in the classical Greek sense of having lost its essential virtue, its *arete*. The virtue of a knife, the *arete* of a knife, is its "cuttingness"; the virtue of a military force is its "fightingness." The U.S. military now stands ready to fight the imagined, preplanned "real war"—that is, the war in Europe—but has no willingness to fight the wars that actually happen, such as that in El Salvador.

The consequences of this is world disequilibrium. International society today is characterized by a sort of perverted Gaullism. But de Gaulle, in his heyday, needed all the strength of his towering figure, and control of a truly major country, to assert a minimum of independence against two terrifically dynamic superpowers. The Soviet Union today, because of the decrepitude of its economy, has lost its dynamism. The Russians can't open new accounts. They can keep Cuba afloat but they can't take on Mozambique. And the United States, because of the consequences of the war that I've described, is mostly passive.

In this perverted Gaullist world, a country need not be led by a de Gaulle to assert its independence. Broad areas of the globe are left unmanaged, to be exploited by regional organizers like South Africa or Syria, which the superpowers can't control. And pirate states—St. Augustine's *magna latrocinia,* great thieveries— such as Qaddafi's Libya thrive. Only recently a ship chartered by the U.S. Navy was attacked by actual pirates in the Strait of Malacca. This is the disequilibrium of the world we live in today. This situation will not last. The question is whether it will be the United States that remedies it; if not, others forces will.

Chace: While Paul Kennedy described an inevitable adjustment of and constraint on American power that followed the Vietnam War but only partly resulted from it, Edward Luttwak is implying that the United States could still function as a world policeman, could still *impose* a kind of *Pax Americana* and countries ranging from South Africa to Syria—if only it had the will. But is such a role possible for any nation any longer?

Luttwak: Apart from the United States, I see no power willing or able to pay this role. The United States is in a transitional stage where the consequences of Vietnam are slowly being absorbed. But I see a clear and logical link between the 1,000 sorties flown each day in Vietnam—which, had they hit worthwhile targets, would have ended the war in a day—and those Marines standing guard outside U.S. battalion headquarters in Beirut who didn't have a single loaded round in their M-16s.

Frances FitzGerald: Whom exactly would you have bombed in Lebanon?

Luttwak: To be an advocate of strategy is not quite the same as being an advocate of frenzied bellicosity in every direction. As it happens, I would not have intervened in Lebanon at all. My point is simply that the United States made a minimum symbolic commitment in Lebanon. During the Marines' mission, Secretary Weinberger advertised his displeasure with their deployment every time he appeared on television. The operational consequence of that reluctance was that the 1,800 Americans were not seen as the point of a wedge that would broaden into a 5,000-or 50,000-man force, if necessary. They were not seen as merely the tangible manifestation of a greater American power but as the affirmation of American impotence. That was the pitiful, helpless giant of Nixon's immortal words, stationed there in Beirut.

FitzGerald: As a matter of fact, I consider that speech of Nixon's—in which he announced the Cambodian incursion—crucial to an understanding of American foreign policy after Vietnam. In that speech, a certain vision of the world is clearly delineated. The alternatives set out are American control over the world, or anarchy and totalitarianism. There is something metaphysical in this vision—particularly as Nixon goes on to say that it is not our power but our will and character that are being tested. Apparently, the United States can restore world order by symbolic action, and by force of character alone. This had now become a familiar theme in American foreign policy; and it is hardly *Realpolitik*, though some present it as such. Nixon is not discussing whether the United States really has the capacity to project its power all over the world; rather, he is discussing the country's character, or virtue.

Mr. Luttwak, what would you prescribe for our policy in El Salvador?

Luttwak: I believe the United States should help the Salvadoran government, which is a democratizing regime, win the war. By "win" I mean reduce the level of guerrilla activity to endemic banditry, which is appropriate to a place of that sort. The United States can permit the Salvadorans to prevail by using their traditional methods—which simply entail killing as many people as they can until there are no guerrillas left. Or, if we insist on imposing our own squeamish tastes on the Salvadorans in typical Yankee imperialist fashion, we must supply them with enough military aid to fight the war cleanly. American methods are clean, but very expensive, requiring helicopters and other sophisticated equipment. The traditional way requires only infantry battalions and plenty of sharp knives. At present we are imposing our mode of warfare on the Salvadorans without funding it sufficiently.

FitzGerald: What is this nonsense about "endemic banditry" and "clean American methods"? It's absurb to look at a situation like that in El Salvador from a purely military point of view. The problem in El Salvador is not the guerrillas but the government—the military-dominated government that actually created the guerrillas and now can't get rid of them without American help. But the kind of help the United States can provide—greater troop mobility and vastly increased firepower—inflicts enormous damage and suffering on the civilian population. The destruction is "clean" only in the sense that it's impersonal.

Karl Marx once said that history repeats itself only as farce. From the point of view of American policy, El Salvador is a farcical replay of Vietnam. The difference is that the Salvadoran guerrillas are very, very vulnerable in a way that the Vietnamese were not, because El Salvador is a small country and it's possible to drive all civilians out of guerrilla-held areas, to drain the water and leave the fish exposed. The evacuation of the guerrilla-held zones is already half accomplished. But it does not solve the political problems of El Salvador.

Luttwak: Look, El Salvador is a tiny country with a few flea-bitten guerrillas. If our country was not traumatized by Vietnam, the whole affair would be concluded very quickly, I assure you.

Kennedy: I wonder about that. If Vietnam had not occurred, and America never experienced the loss of morale and the feelings of insecurity the war brought with it, I still doubt that, at this point, the United States would be able to go in and *solve* the conflict in El Salvador, or *solve* problems in other Third World countries.

Peter Marin: I think we're ignoring another significant constraint on American power emerging from the war: the political pressures that seem to restrict America's foreign, and especially military, policies. Something extraordinary and, I think, quite wonderful happened in this country during the Vietnam War—a large part of the population refused to accept the government's announced policy. What you take to be a loss of morale seems to me to be a kind of growing up. One must not forget that by the end of the war, elected officials were able to govern only by shooting people in the streets, or threatening to.

One of the major constraints on American policy is the lingering fear—conscious or unconsious—on the part of those in authority that a similar crisis could erupt if certain kinds of policies are implemented. We now have in the United States a military and political policy constrained, at least in part, by the feelings of its citizens, feelings based on remembered experience rather than on propaganda.

Kevin P. Phillips: I'm not sure American public opinion is the constraint you think it is. Let's look at some recent foreign-policy controversies to see if what you say holds true. First, there was the acrimonious debate over the Panama Canal Treaties in 1977 and 1978. The treaties were widely condemned in this country, and I think that was a measure of Americans' frustration with their country's diminished role in the world after Vietnam and their rejection of what appeared to be a retreat in Central and South America. Related feelings, I think, lay behind the public's anger with President Carter's inability to exercise American power effectively during the Iranian hostage crisis.

But consider the reaction to the Grenada invasion—Americans expressed enormous pleasure at this exercise of U.S. power, even though it was used only to invade a little tinpot country. Their pleasure was enough to kick up President Reagan's approval rating about ten points overnight. The public is completely amenable to an *effective* display of American power.

FitzGerald: But at what cost? Grenada is a small, pathetic place; it was possible to "conquer" the island quickly with very few casualties. Would Americans support interventions where the costs were not quite so small?

The problem here is partly that, as Professor Kennedy said, during the last twenty years the United States has had to face revolutionary changes in the Third World. During the fifties, when most Third World countries were still governed by very small groups of elites and the great masses of people were uninvolved in their national politics, it was easy for the United States to overthrow what it considered an undesirable government. In 1954, the United States was able to overthrow the Arbenz government in Guatemala in a few weeks by means of a secret, inexpensive, and relatively painless CIA operation. In Iran, the year before, a single CIA agent was able to restore the Shah to his throne in a matter of three days.

But small-scale and painless interventions are practically impossible these days. The recent upheaval in Iran, in which a small, American-backed ruling elite was violently overthrown—and which was prefigured to some extent by the U.S. defeat in Vietnam—has been repeated in less dramatic form in many Third World countries. Even in a tiny country like El Salvador, the United States is finding it must exert an enormous effort and inflict hideous pain on the local population just to ensure that its allies remain in power.

I don't believe Americans are interested in such costly interventions, however much they enjoyed the symbolism of Grenada. But many in this country have not quite accepted the changes in the Third World as a part of reality, a part of the world as it is. They picture a bipolar world in which only the United States and the Soviet Union have any real power and Third World countries are essentially amenable to manipulation by whoever gets there first.

Luttwak: When we talk about the Third World, I think it's important not to replace the outdated conception of the 1960s—which saw the Third World as completely malleable when in fact it was becoming less so—with one that is already becoming outdated. Many Third World nations are again becoming receptive to American influence. U.S. forces in El Salvador, for example, don't evoke a negative reaction from people whose greatest ambition is to emigrate to the United States. For a good number of Salvadorans, McDonald's is an ideal.

Obviously there is greater resistance in more strongly defined cultures—like the Islamic culture—that are now in decay. If the young men in these countries desert the mosques, they do so to read *Playboy,* not *Pravda.* So it is perfectly rational for the Islamic fundamentalists to see the United States as their principal threat. Their very extremism stems from their sense of imminent cultural collapse. They fear that if they don't follow the Western model they'll simply rot, culturally and intellectually.

FitzGerald: Given your analysis, one might wonder why it has proved so difficult for the United States to defeat "a few flea-bitten guerrillas" in El Salvador. On the other hand, the United States is not seen as the only threat to the Islamic world. In Afghanistan, the Russians are being resisted with great intensity, as is the Soviet model. The Third World's, and especially the Islamic world's, reaction to the Soviet invasion has been instructive. So it does seem to matter who gets there first.

Luttwak: Behind the Soviet helicopters there are no McDonald's. That is a consideration.

Chace: It seems to me that Lebanon is a good example of a country, once strongly pro-Western, that has undergone some of the upheavals Frances FitzGerald described. In his summary of the American public's reaction to recent foreign-policy controversies, I don't believe Mr. Phillips mentioned the Reagan Administration's intervention in Lebanon, which no one could perceive as a success, either strategically or in terms of public opinion.

Phillips: But the failure in Lebanon was not held against the Administration. Why? Because Americans do not associate this Administration with the retreat of American power. However ineptly or ineffectively he may have applied that power in Lebanon, President Reagan was able to wrap the Star Spangled Banner around himself—simply because he has always opposed the idea that the United States should acquiesce to indigenous challenges in the Third World.

Chace: In other words, the failure in Beirut was covered over by rhetoric.

Phillips: Such failures often are. The point is that the political opportunities for blaming Reagan were virtually nonexistent because he had cultivated an image of strength.

Marin: That Americans love an *image* of strength is not being contested here. Whether that means they would accept another 50,000 dead in a foreign intervention is another question. No one has mentioned those 50,000 dead. I don't believe the war can be fully understood if it is regarded only as a strategic defeat; the war was also a traumatic event in the lives of actual men and women. We have to consider the American people's perception of the suffering we inflicted on others and the suffering at least some Americans experienced directly. After all, the war was perceived by many Americans not just as a military defeat but as a moral defeat, or at least a moral error.

What do people do when they have not only been defeated militarily but also believe they have been defeated morally? How does a country like ours, with its mythical sense of itself as a force for good in the world, deal with a moral defeat, a moral tragedy? These questions have been pushed beneath the surface during the last ten years—and I believe the fact that they are there, unacknowledged, has colored our foreign policy much more than the military defeat *per se* has.

Phillips: Actually, the United States has a long pathology of postwar reaction. After wars, Americans tend to blame dissidents, and political parties, for unpatriotic behavior. The Federalist Party was crushed after the War of 1812, in which it had been seen as giving aid and comfort to the British; the Whigs were undercut by their opposition to the Mexican War; after World War I there was a large-scale crackdown on antiwar dissidents and radicals. And McCarthyism was in some measure a means to allocate blame for the "loss" of Eastern Europe and China as a result of what were perceived to be weak Democratic policies.

Marin: Yes, but when Americans are confronted with the *reality* of defeat, they tend to reassert their old myths. That is what seems to be happening under Reagan, who presents an *image* of power while avoiding those confrontations that might put it to a test—which, in my view, is precisely why Americans like him.

Luttwak: I would like to step back from this debate on public opinion to point out that the purpose of strategy in foreign policy is not to recognize and infinitely adapt to change, but to maintain a set of values and interests by *resisting* change. Any empire is a great machine of conservation against change—that is the nature of empire. Thus to say that because the Third World is becoming more independent, we automatically must do such is not strategy.

Kennedy: Of course all great powers are essentially conservative—they've risen to the top and don't want to be thrown off. But it's necessary for them to find ways of responding to challenges to their position with some degree of subtlety. Sometimes, of course, such challenges must be resisted. But if an empire is completely ethnocentric, if all it can see is a world filtered through its own strategic concerns, then its chances of misreading the situation in a country—of standing firm where it isn't a good idea to stand firm, or of not standing firm where it is—are that much greater.

George Gilder: But the fact remains that support around the world for the American system has in fact increased since Vietnam. To see this clearly we have only to look at the world economically, instead of geopolitically. If we consider the economic consequences of Vietnam, I think we'll see that there's a real sense in which the United States won the Vietnam War. At least we won the one prize that was worth anything—the boat people. The boat people are now key figures in the high-tech companies in Silicon Valley and across the country, and are thus contributing substantially to American economic growth.

America's victory in Vietnam is more evident when we look at our economy's growing dominance in the world. At the end of the war, our gross domestic product was a quarter of the world's output; for 1984 it is estimated at almost a third. And the predominance of the capitalist system is nowhere more dramatic than in Asia. The communists may continue to dominate the pathetic small places, but less pathetic small places—Singapore, Hong Kong, Taiwan—are booming capitalist countries.

This massive shift in economic power from the communist world to the capitalist world, symbolized by the boat people, has been far more important than the tactical defeat the United States suffered in Vietnam. America's position in the world has steadily improved in the last decade. And it will keep improving if we continue the emancipation of our economy that President Reagan has begun—recapturing the momentum the Kennedy Administration began with its tax cut. The Vietnam War was a crucial factor in this economic development, because in the 1960s, partly to pay for the war, the government started raising tax rates again. There was economic devastation for several years because of Vietnam. But as soon as the war was over, as soon as tax rates were cut, the United States began to demonstrate that it could again dominate the world economically—which is the way that counts.

Indeed, perhaps the most harmful consequence of Vietnam was that it helped reinforce the fallacy of geopolitics—the idea that the cold war is about real estate, that it really makes a different to America's power that the Russians control Afghanistan or Angola or Ethiopia, all those pathetic countries you can't even visit without getting sick.

Luttwak: Such as Transylvania, where I happen to have been born.

Gilder: Well, maybe you have emotional ties to Transylvania. But in the long run you're probably much more valuable to the United States.

Chace: Perhaps this is the point where, after discussing the war's effects on the American military, and after touching on its economic consequences, we should take up the question of America's "vital interests." In fact, Vietnam was always of marginal strategic importance to the United States. Another consequence of the war, surely, has been a continuing debate about what we actually mean by an American vital interest. President Reagan, for example, defined Lebanon as a vital interest, but our withdrawal from Beirut does not seem to have hurt the United States. How do we define what this country's vital interests are?

Luttwak: When an empire loses a vital interest, it's supposed to collapse. If the empire doesn't collapse, then what it lost wasn't a vital interest.

Marin: I think the problem has to do with how we see ourselves. Everyone here keeps using the word "empire," assuming that the United States must intervene all over the globe or else fade into insignificance. There is obviously a lot of room in between; yet Americans don't have any images or theories to help them describe their country's role in the world—to explain themselves *to* themselves. We have a sense of defeat, I believe, not simply because the American empire seems to be falling apart, but because once we can no longer see ourselves as a great empire, we don't know how to see ourselves.

Gilder: I think the Vietnam War did vindicate a certain world view—that of the American right. No one talks about this much, of course, but our retreat from Vietnam led to a holocaust, a stream of atrocities that consumed all of Indochina—which was precisely what the right had warned would happen. That holocaust allowed the rest of the world to see clearly what happens when a country is lost to communism, and it is bound to make other countries more willing to resist communism on their own.

Marin: That's much too simple a view. The effects of Vietnam are more tragic, and less ideological, that that. Many Americans are smart enough to realize that while our withdrawal from Vietnam had certain tragic consequences, our presence, had we remained there, would have led to a different, and equally tragic, set of consequences. This knowledge is the difficulty: we understand that both America's presence and its absence have had consequences of which we despair. And no one on the left or right has managed to do much with this knowledge, other than to assert over and over the weakness of the other side's position.

Luttwak: But empires shouldn't have to use military force to secure their interests in the first place. Empires secure their interests by *not* using military force; they rely on their reputation for using force only when it is absolutely needed, and then in an utterly implacable manner. If you're in the empire business, it is your duty to be implacable when somebody opposes you—especially when the conflict is on a small scale, and terminating it is nice and cheap. The problem is that the American people never really saw their country as an imperial power; the United States was not designed to manage an empire.

Gilder: America is not in the empire business; the Russians are. But the Soviet Union's economy is steadily declining. The Russian's can't even feed themselves. The country is a total failure, a pitiful, helpless giant in every respect except the ability to build up military power. Everything outside the military sphere is going in the United States' direction, beyond the greatest expectations anyone had in the 1950s or 1960s. Today socialism is a joke. Nobody believes in it as a workable economic paradigm anymore. The dynamic has definitely shifted; soon our military strategies will develop to the point where they will properly complement the resurgence of American power and capitalist domination.

Kennedy: But the war in Vietnam, along with the massive outpouring of *vox populi* to end the fighting, lent new prominence and seriousness to the ongoing debate over what the country's vital interests really are. Of course, many other countries, great empires and small, have asked these questions of themselves—What are our vital interests? When should we fight for them? But usually the debate has taken place secretly, within an elite group of rulers. It is much more difficult to define your vital interests in a public forum without at the same time letting your adversaries know where you will stand and fight and where you will not. I think that was a big part of the problem in Lebanon; Secretary of Defense Weinberger and the Joint Chiefs were afraid of getting bogged down—and the secretary said so publicly. Since Vietnam, the military has been hypercautious because it has not devised an effective way to analyze America's vital interests and priorities in public. The public debate—as well as the constant leaks about the private debates—makes managing a global system of influence and interests extraordinarily difficult.

Luttwak: A nation can overcome some of the problems you mentioned simply by advertising clearly to its people, and to the world, a general willingness to defend areas that are strategically or economically important to it. To point to specific places is to be *un*-strategical—an empire doesn't protect its interests by fighting all over the world; rather, it discourages other nations from taking action against it by responding decisively and implacably when it absolutely must.

Kennedy: Yet it is much easier for a nation to be predictable and implacable in defense of its interests when it has a government and a military designed to carry out sustained overseas wars. A small professional army and a nondemocratic system of government enable a nation to maintain an empire. But a full-blown democracy with a conscript mass army—which is what America was at the time of the Vietnam War—will have an extraordinarily difficult time repeatedly going to war to keep recalcitrant natives down. For that, we need a quite different military structure and a quite different constitution.

Marin: Which leads us to another important consequence of Vietnam: the war forced many Americans to recognize the caste nature of their army—who went to war and who did not. Americans began to notice that their country's conscript army was drawn from the lower middle class and the working class—the young men who didn't go to college. And this knowledge in turn made people more resistant to authority and suspicious of elites who might lead them to war. The war also showed Americans that one could refuse to fight without anything terrible happening. It's difficult to administer an empire if, in the midst of a war, people are able and willing to say: We don't want to fight.

Chace: Mr. Phillips, how do you assess the war's effect on American politics?

Phillips: Of course, the impact of Vietnam has dominated American politics for the last decade. The most obvious consequence of the war was the radicalization of the Democratic Party and the shift of the patriotic image to the Republicans. This has allowed the Republicans to control the political debate since 1968, except for the interval of Watergate. Watergate, which was clearly tied very closely to Vietnam, destabilized the Nixon/Ford regime and helped elect Jimmy Carter, who could have reached the presidency only after a scandal that enabled him to run as the Sunday school candidate preaching a government of love and trust.

I think Vietnam and Watergate together distorted the underlying political trends of the last fifteen years. Instead of the orderly advance of the moderate conservative political cycle that started in the late 1960s, there was an aberrant interruption of it—in the person of Jimmy Carter—followed by a more extreme repackaging of conservatism under Ronald Reagan. I say extreme because this Administration, in its foreign policy at least, appeals to Americans who long for the simpler days of overwhelming American power. But the country can't return to the good old days, so Americans glory in the conquest of Grenada—just as Britain, that old empire with *its* nostalgic government, gloried in its conquest of the Falklands.

Marin: But here we come back to the social dimension of Vietnam that no one seems to want to discuss. American authority was exposed as incompetent and corrupt. Our soldiers refused to fight.

Our intelligence agents denounced their government and revealed CIA crimes. Our leaders were shown to be scheming criminals. Day after day, the front page of the evening newspaper, the first few minutes of the evening news, told Americans about the stupidity and dishonesty of their government. Americans, in short, found themselves unable to see the emperor's clothes any longer, whether they wanted to or not. And what they did see, I believe, is still bothering them today, even though many of them seem to be struggling mightily to forget it.

Luttwak: Irving Kristol has a theory about this, which explains these events as part of the classic demoralization of the elites in power. According to Kristol, these elites were eventually undermined by another group—the so-called new class of journalists, publicists, academics, and advertising men.

Marin: Look, I'm trying to talk about the effect of the Vietnam War on the American people. Define what happened as a result of a struggle among elites, if you like. But obviously the war had an enormous effect on the populace at large.

Luttwak: Sure it did. The populace at large reacted by shouting, "We want Ronald Reagan!"

Marin: It is extraordinarily simplistic to treat the American public as if it were one great reactive animal. In order to understand the social effects of the war we have to examine the different groups in our society. For instance, the war had a different effect on the left than on the right. The off thing was that the left was more demoralized by the cupidity of power than the right; it was as if those on the left learned that what they had been saying for so long about authority and power in America was true, and yet they found themselves unable to do anything with this confirmation.

Phillips: It's true the war crippled the right and the left in different ways. Liberals and others on the left find it impossible even now to come to grips with the question of the effective use of American power. For the voters, the upheavals surrounding the war served to gather together a whole cluster of issues that were widely unpopular, at least in Middle America—what were considered permissive attitudes toward crime and education, and disrespectful attitudes toward patriotism—and to identify them closely with reform elements within the Democratic Party. That radicalization of the party, combined with the weakness of its old elites and the dramatic new assertiveness of minorities, tremendously enfeebled the Democrats.

The Republicans, meanwhile have been able to use the patriotism issue effectively since 1968. But Vietnam crippled conservatives as well, in a different sense, giving them a rather warped, nostalgic view of American power and a simplistic view of recent American history. They cling to the belief that America can pull the world together again, as it did under Eisenhower. I thnk that's an illusion, with little basis in the political and economic facts of the world we live in today.

Kennedy: But how long do you think these political effects will be felt? Today I see on the campuses a different generation, for whom the war and the bitter battles that were fought over it are ancient history. I wonder if we're not really talking about attitudes that are held strongly by one or two generations, but that have not been absorbed by the larger culture.

Marin: Perhaps. It may well be that a couple of American generations experienced in this war, at least in a small way, something akin to what Europeans suffered in World War I. Vietnam drove home to Americans that war is *tragic*. Vietnam was as close as modern war has ever come to the United States. The number of men who served, the embittered veterans, the nightly television news, the violent demonstrations in our streets—all this ensured that the war would have an extraordinary impact on the American imagination. Hundreds of books have been written about the war—not books about policy or strategy, but books about horror, about terror, about shame.

Gilder: And that obsessive attitude toward the war so paralyzed the Vietnam generation that it couldn't participate effectively in the American economy for many years. These people just sat around smoking pot and fantasizing about fascist "Amerika."

The new generation on the rise sees not violence on our campuses but the Chinese Communist leaders declaring that Marxism is dead—which happens to be immensely more important than any consequence of Vietnam. It is clear by now that the notion that America was losing authority in the world, that it was being overwhelmed by some inexorable trend exemplified by Vietnam, was plain wrong.

Marin: The Vietnam War was a moral event, and you're incapable of providing anything but an economic response to it. Americans have no means to describe the moral experience of Vietnam. This experience has been lost; or rather, it has become subterranean, and will probably remain so because we have no language to bring it to the surface. This failure of language was the great problem of the left—whatever lessons it learned it turned into hysteria, rather than into wisdom. And this explains, partly, the upsurge of the new privilege George Gilder mentioned—the right simply had no other response to the events that happened during the war. So the left remains mute, and the right grows increasingly self-righteous and trivial in its concerns. That's an immense waste. We could perhaps have become a wiser people. But the war is an experience that is not becoming part of the collective wisdom.

Gilder: Americans are getting on with their lives, in other words.

Marin: Yes, but perhaps at the expense of our children. We must not "get on with our lives" without coming to terms with what happened in the war.

FitzGerald: I believe that America's reaction to the war has been solipsistic, in several ways. First, Vietnam veterans have a deep sense that their government victimized them by sending them off on a venture that the society, in the end, didn't approve of. The war was undertaken to achieve aims that were totally unclear to those who fought it, and which turned out never to have existed at all. I don't think this sense of victimization has been overcome. But it has remained a psychological issue for the veterans; it has never really been transformed into a politics. Look at the novels that have come out of Vietnam. They're all intensely personal. There has been no novel of any political scope about Vietnam since Graham Greene wrote *The Quiet American*. There's been no *Catch-22*, no attempt at such a comprehensive political understanding on the part of any veteran, or any novelist for that matter.

Americans still prefer to treat Vietnam as a psychological problem for veterans—post-Vietnam syndrome. We can't seem to *see* the war as a political problem. And the analyses of what post-

Vietnam foreign policy should be seem to me similarly solipsistic. No one can come to grips with the fact that none of the objectives the United States imagined it had going into the war justified the size and the ultimate cost of the commitment. What finally happened when we were defeated, when we lost the war? Nothing. Our defeat left our vaunted national security interests in Asia essentially unharmed; indeed, the United States today is arguably in a better position in Asia than it ever has been.

So what *did* we lose? The right usually answers with more psychological propositions: Vietnam was a failure of will, a failure of nerve. Apparently their concern is that the American image was damaged. But what is that except a sort of narcissistic mortification? The war has not prompted a realistic, reasonable debate about what America's foreign-policy goals are; rather, it has prompted violent swings of emotion over ridiculous symbols. The Grenada invasion was a perfect example of such a symbol—an event of no real consequence that caused an enormous emotional outpouring in this country. So now America is "standing tall" again. The only serious foreign-policy question that has been asked as a result of Vietnam is "Where can the United States intervene militarily?" Surely there are more important questions to ask about the goals of American foreign policy than that.

Luttwak: The questions about American foreign policy after Vietnam certainly will not be answered by pondering Grenada. To answer those questions we have to look at Europe.

During the war, it was the hope of the left that America's eventual defeat would bring to an end the assertion of American power worldwide. The left hoped we would withdraw from Europe and Korea and our other primary commitments abroad, thus enabling the world to achieve a new equilibrium where good leftist regimes would run the show. But the mainstream consensus about America's role in the world was not smashed by our withdrawal from Vietnam; in large part the common sense of the American people prevailed, although there is more disagreement than before about peripheral interests. But when we talk about America's role in the world, we are talking first of all about Europe; and there the question is not military intervention but our presence in Germany, which continues to link the fate of America to what happens along the border between the two Germanys. That's why when we talk about America "projecting its power abroad," we are really talking about piddling little areas that are not central to the debate.

Marin: We must not forget that there exists a realm between the political and the psychological. We need to define what the terms of a moral debate would be—that is, what consequences justify what costs? For instance, some estimates of the number of vets who committed suicide after the war are as high as 50,000. Americans have never confronted this fact. And it has not been ignored because of our wonderful economic situation and the rise of the yuppies. We have evaded it, because recognizing it would demand so much of us. What does it mean to America that after this war, 50,000 ex-soldiers committed suicide? And what does it mean that our nation won't confront this?

Gilder: There we have a vivid demonstration of the solipsism of the left on the subject of Vietnam—the notion that all Vietnam veterans are somehow traumatized by guilt. In fact, most of them are very proud of their participation in the war; it's the people who evaded the draft who are suffering traumas of guilt. By pointing to all this supposed psychological damage, the left is attempting to show that its opposition to the war has been vindicated.

Luttwak: The suicides were a result of the fact that the elite presented the war in a manner designed to humiliate those who fought in it, to make their sacrifice seem unworthy.

Marin: It is truly corrupt to take this fact and turn it into a political argument. Why should we assume that all the vets committed suicide for precisely the same reason? What you describe was one reason, but there were many others.

Gilder: Such as drug abuse.

Marin: Such as shame and humiliation. I know vets who think it was a wonderful war and were deeply enraged by the reception they got when they came home. But there are many vets, perhaps far more, who can't get over their guilt. Let me give you a very simple example: a vet who can't forget that at the beginning of the war, he threw cans of food to children from the backs of trucks because he wanted to feed them, and that by the end of the war, he was *pelting* the children with the cans, trying to *kill* them. He says he will spend the rest of his life trying to find a way to atone for that.

Now, he doesn't feel shame about America's role in the war or the loss of the war; he feels shame about what he himself did during the war. And our inability to recognize this adds to his shame.

Kennedy: The argument I've been witnessing for the last few minutes seems to me a consequence of Vietnam: an almost unbridgeable divide has been created in the political culture of this country.

I recently attended a conference on Anglo-American relations. During the proceedings, one of the Brits mentioned the Suez intervention in 1956, whereupon another Brit jumped to his feet and violently disagreed with him. Then several others joined in. The entire conference stopped dead for ten minutes while this group of Brits of a particular generation quarreled about Suez. This explosion was a startling reminder of what the impact of Suez had been at the time; it was an event which sent shock waves through the British body politic.

The Vietnam War had an even more violent impact on the Americans who lived through it. It enormously intensified political and ideological feelings, and some Americans will never stop quarreling about it—about the appropriate use of military force, about whether it is moral or not moral for America to intervene abroad, about whether a democracy can truly manage an empire. All of these political disagreements extend outward from the sort of arguments we've heard around this table today.

Marin: The quarrel, I fear, involves far more than political differences. It involves a disagreement about how men and women, and nations, ought to measure their actions. The vets I know best, for instance, are Catholics, the good boys who went to war because their leaders and priests told them to fight godless communism. Many of them now feel enormous guilt at having done things for which they find themselves unable to atone. The priests in Vietnam came to bless their guns rather than to give them counsel or comfort or genuine help in coming to terms with their actions. This turned many of these vets against the church in the end: they could no longer depend on it to guide them in their lives.

A crisis concerning the proper moral basis for actions and decisions was coming in America anyway, but the war precipitated it, brought it to the surface. The same kinds of complex ethical questions raised by the war are at work in the abortion controversy and the debate about Baby Doe. After all, what we are talking about here is *killing*. We are discussing when and where the state, or individual men and women, have a legitimate right to accomplish their ends by taking thousands of lives, or even, for that matter, a single life.

What we are talking about, in short, is the value of human life, and this is not merely a political or legal issue. It points, as do the other disagreements around this table, both to the complexities of moral choice now confronting us and to a tremendous confusion about the nature of moral life itself. This, I believe, more than any political controversy, explains the power the war still exerts upon us.

Chace: Finally, we have to ask: Has the American myth, so damaged by Vietnam, really been reconstructed? Perhaps "reconstructing the myth" is a prejudicial phrase; it might be simpler to ask, Has the *idea* of America, pre-Vietnam America, been reconstructed? The America that can bless a war as it has in the past, that can take firm action in the belief that it is acting rightly, that formulates policy in the belief that it is fulfilling a right and proper mission in the world? Or has this America been set aside— and if so, for how long?

Phillips: In all likelihood, the effects of Vietnam will be pervasive in the United States so long as the generation that was in its early and mid-twenties at the war's height holds sway in American society. And that generation, is just assuming power. Through this generation, Vietnam will continue as a subliminal disability in American politics and American society—saddling the left with a paralyzing inablility to come to grips with the use of American power abroad, pushing the right to pursue a nostalgic re-creation of an all-powerful America drawn from another era, and, in general, undercutting all attempts to achieve consensus in American foreign policy.

Chace: We have certainly seen here today that while Ronald Reagan's America may be an assertive America, a resurgent

America, it is not an undivided America. The foreign and domestic consensus that largely made possible the forceful exercise of American power after World War II was broken by Vietnam and has never been put back together again. Vietnam was the beginning of the end of the American dream of limitless expectations—we lost our first war.

Without such a consensus, managing a coherent and effective foreign policy is terribly difficult. More to the point, U.S. military intervention abroad, without a clear-cut threat to the United States proper, becomes nearly impossible to carry out. It is not simply a question of military power; the moral and political backing for such intervention, which is imperative in a country such as ours, is lacking.

Without a shared set of moral and political values, how can we agree on what should be defended and with what means? From what we have heard today, it is hard not to conclude that while the image of a self-confident America may well be in the making, the reality remains very different.

THE MEANING OF VIETNAM[4]

Just a few hundred yards from here stands the Vietnam Veterans Memorial. Its stark beauty is a reminder of the searing experience our country went through in its longest war. From a window of my office I can see the crowds of people—veterans, families, old and young—coming to search for names on the black granite slabs, or to search their souls in meditation. It is more than a memorial; it is a living human tribute taking place day after day. This is not surprising. That war left its mark on all the American people.

There are three dozen names that do not appear on that memorial. Instead, they are here in this diplomatic entrance, on our own roll of honor. Many civilians served in Southeast Asia—from

[4]Reprint of an address at the Department of State, on April 25, 1985, by George P. Shultz, U. S. Secretary of State. *Department of State Bulletin.* 85: 13–16. Je. '85. Copyright © by the Department of State. Reprinted by permission.

the State Department, AID [Agency for International Development], USIA [United States Information Agency], and other agencies. Many of you here today were among them. While the war raged, you were trying to build peace—working for land reform, for public health and economic progress, for constitutional development, for public information, for a negotiated end to the war. I am here to pay tribute to you.

The 10th anniversary of the fall of Indochina is an occasion for all of us, as a nation, to reflect on the meaning of that experience. As the fierce emotions of that time subside, perhaps our country has a better chance now of assessing the war and its impact. This is not merely a historical exercise. Our understanding of the past affects our conduct in the present, and thus, in part, determines our future.

Let me discuss what has happened in Southeast Asia, and the world, since 1975; what light those postwar events shed on the war itself; and what relevance all this has to our foreign policy today.

Indochina since 1975

The first point—and it stands out for all to see—is that the communist subjection of Indochina has fulfilled the worst predictions of the time. The bloodshed and misery that communist rule wrought in South Vietnam, and in Cambodia and Laos, add yet another grim chapter to the catalog of agony of the 20th century.

Since 1975, over 1 million refugees have fled South Vietnam to escape the new tyranny. In 1978, Hanoi decided to encourage the flight of refugees by boat. At its height in the spring of 1979, the exodus of these "boat people" reached over 40,000 a month. Tens, perhaps hundreds, of thousands never made it to safety and today lie beneath the South China Sea. Others managed to survive pirate attacks and other hardships at sea in their journey to freedom. We have welcomed more than 730,000 Indochinese refugees to our shores. The work of people in this Department has saved countless lives. Your dedication to the refugees of Indochina marks one of the shining moments of the Foreign Service.

In addition to "boat people," Hanoi has given the world its own version of the "reeducation camp." When the North Viet-

namese Army conquered the south, it rounded up officials and
supporters of the South Vietnamese Government, as well as other
suspected opponents. Many were executed or disappeared forever.
Hundreds of thousands were sent to these camps, suffering hard
labor, indoctrination, and violent mistreatment. To this day, up-
ward of 10,000 remain imprisoned. They include Buddhist and
Christian clergy and intellectuals, as well as former political figures. According to refugee reports, they face indeterminate sen-
tences, receive food rations below subsistence levels, are denied
basic medical care, and are punished severely for even minor in-
fractions of camp rules—punishment often resulting in permanent
injury or death.

Hanoi has asserted for years that it will let these prisoners go
if only we would take them all. Last fall, President Reagan offered
to bring all genuine political prisoners to freedom in the United
States. Now, Hanoi no longer adheres to its original proposal.

Another communist practice has been to relocate people in so-
called new economic zones. In the years after the fall of Saigon,
hundreds of thousands were uprooted and forced into these isolated and barren rural areas to expand agricultural production and
reduce "unproductive" urban populations. Many have fled the
zones, returning to the cities to live in hiding, without the ration
or neighborhood registration cards needed to get food or jobs. Indeed, no one in Vietnam may change residence or place of work
without permission, and unauthorized absences open whole families to arrest.

The 24 million people of South Vietnam are now victims of
a totalitarian state, before which they stand naked without the
protection of a single human right. As Winston Churchill said of
another communist state, they have been "frozen in an indefinite
winter of subhuman doctrine and superhuman tyranny."

Compare conditions in Vietnam under 10 years of communist
rule with conditions in the South Vietnam we fought to defend.
The South Vietnamese Government accepted the principles of free
elections, freedom of speech, of the press, and of association. From
1967 to 1971 the South Vietnamese people voted in nine elections;
opposition parties played a major role in the assembly. Before
1975 there were 27 daily newspapers, some 200 journals of opin-

ion and scholarship, 3 television and 2 dozen radio stations, all operating in relative freedom.

No, South Vietnam was not a Jeffersonian democracy with full civil liberties by American standards. But there was a vigorous, pluralist political process, and the government intruded little into the private lives of the people. They enjoyed religious freedom and ethnic tolerance, and there were few restrictions on cultural or intellectual life. The transgressions of the Thieu government pale into insignificance next to the systematic, ideologically impelled despotism of the regime that replaced it.

The neutralist government in neighboring Laos was swiftly taken over in 1975 by local communists loyal to Hanoi. As in Vietnam, thousands of former officials were sent to "reeducation camps." Fifty thousand Vietnamese troops remain in Laos to ensure the "irreversibility" of communist control—in Hanoi's version of the Brezhnev doctrine—and thousands of Vietnamese advisers are in place to monitor Laos' own "socialist transformation."

Hmong villagers in Laos who resisted communist control were suppresed by a military juggernaut that relied on chemical weapons produced and supplied by the Soviet Union in violation of international treaties. Six decades of international restraints on chemical warfare have been dangerously eroding in recent years, and "yellow rain" in Indochina was the first major breach—yellow rain, another addition to our vocabulary from post-1975 Indochina.

Finally, in Cambodia, the worst horror of all: the genocide of at least 1 million Cambodians by the Khmer Rouge, who also took power 10 years ago this month. The Khmer Rouge emptied the cities and murdered the educated; they set out to destroy traditional Cambodian society and to construct a wholly new and "pure" society on the ruins of the old. A French Jesuit who witnessed the early phases of communist rule called it "a perfect example of the application of an ideology pushed to the furthest limit of its internal logic." We say at least 1 million dead. Maybe it was 2 million. The suffering and misery represented by such numbers are beyond our ability to comprehend. Our imaginations are confined by the limits of the civilized life we know.

In December 1978, Vietnam went to war with its erstwhile partners and overthrew the Khmer Rouge regime. Naturally, some Cambodians at first welcomed the Vietnamese as liberators. But as the Vietnamese invaders came to apply in Cambodia the techniques of repression known all too well to the people of Vietnam, resistance in Cambodia grew.

In 1979, Cambodia was ravaged by widespread famine that killed tens, if not hundreds, of thousands. Vietnam bears much responsibility for this famine. Its invasion prevented the planting of the 1979 rice crop; its army adopted scorched-earth tactics in pursuing the retreating Khmer Rouge. Many will recall how the Vietnamese obstructed international relief programs and refused to cooperate with the efforts of the Red Cross and others to establish a "land bridge" of trucks to bring relief into the country from Thailand.

Today, Cambodia is ruled by a puppet regime stiffened by a cadre of hundreds of former Khmer Rouge; it is headed by Heng Samrin, a former Khmer Rouge himself. The Vietnamese shell refugee camps along the Thai border in their attempt to smash the resistance.

Hanoi's leaders are thus extending their rule to the full boundaries of the former colonial domain, seeking dominion over all of Indochina. Not only do the Vietnamese threaten Thailand—the Soviets, with naval and air bases at Cam Ranh Bay, are now better able to project their power in the Pacific, Southeast Asian, and Indian Ocean regions and to threaten vital Western lines of communication in all these regions. Cam Ranh is now the center of the largest concentration of Soviet naval units outside the U.S.S.R.

Retrospective: The Moral Issue

What does all this mean? Events since 1975 shed light on the past: this horror was precisely what we were trying to prevent. The President has called our effort a noble cause, and he was right. Whatever mistakes in how the war was fought, whatever one's view of the strategic rationale for our intervention, the *morality* of our effort must now be clear. Those Americans who served, or who grieve for their loved ones lost or missing, can hold

their heads high: our sacrifice was in the service of noble ideals—
to save innocent people from brutal tyranny. Ellsworth Bunker
used to say: no one who dies for freedom ever dies in vain.

We owe all our Vietnam veterans a special debt. They fought
with courage and skill under more difficult conditions than Americans in any war before them. They fought with a vague and un-
certain mission against a tenacious enemy. They fought knowing
that part of the nation opposed their efforts. They suffered abuse
when they came home. But like their fathers before them, they
fought for what Americans have always fought for: freedom, human dignity, and justice. They are heroes. They honored their
country, and we should show them our gratitude.

And when we speak of honor and gratitude, we speak again
of our prisoners of war—and of the nearly 2,500 men who remain
missing. We will not rest until we have received the fullest possible
accounting of the fate of these heroes.

Retrospective: The Strategic Price

We left Indochina in 1975, but the cost of failure was high.
The price was paid, in the first instance, by the more than 30 mil-
lion people we left behind to fall under communist rule. But
America, and the world, paid a price.

Our domestic divisions weakened us. The war consumed precious defense resources, and the assault on defense spending at
home compounded the cost; years of crucial defense investment
were lost, while the Soviets continued the steady military buildup
they launched after the Cuban missile crisis. These wasted years
are what necessitated our recent defense buildup to restore the
global balance.

For a time, the United States retreated into introspection, self-
doubt, and hesitancy. Some Americans tended to think that
American power was the source of the world's problems, and that
the key to peace was to limit *our* actions in the world. So we imposed all sorts of restrictions on ourselves. Vietnam—and Watergate—left a legacy of congressional restrictions on presidential
flexibility, now embedded in our legislation. Not only the War
Powers Resolution but a host of constraints on foreign aid, arms

exports, intelligence activities, and other aspects of policy—these
weakened the ability of the President to act and to conduct foreign
policy, and they weakened our country. Thus we pulled back from
global leadership.

Our retreat created a vacuum that was exploited by our adversaries. The Soviets concluded that the global "correlation of
forces" was shifting in their favor. They took advantage of our in-
hibitions and projected their power to unprecedented lengths: in-
tervening in Angola, in Ethiopia, in South Yemen, and in
Afghanistan. The Iranian hostage crisis deepened our humiliation.

American weakness turned out to be the most *destabilizing*
factor on the global scene. The folly of isolationism was again revealed. Once again it was demonstrated—the hard way—that
American engagement, American strength, and American leadership are indispensable to peace. A strong America makes the
world a safer place.

Where We Are Today

Today, there are some more positive trends. In Asia, the contrast between communist Indochina and the rest of the region is
striking. Indochina is an economic wreck; the countries of ASEAN
[Association of South East Asian Nations] are advancing economically. In 1982, their per capita income averaged $770; Vietnam's
was $160. ASEAN is a model of regional cooperation. It is now
our fifth largest trading partner. In the past 5 years, total U.S.
trade with East Asia and the Pacific surpassed our trade with any
other region of the world. Our relations with Japan remain excellent and our ties with China are expanding. The regional picture
is clouded by the growing Soviet military presence and by Vietnam's continuing aggression. But a sense of community among the
Pacific nations is growing. A decade after the war, America is re-
storing its position in Asia.

At home, the United States is recovering its economic and military strength. We have overcome the economic crisis of the 1970s
and once again are enjoying economic growth with stable prices.
We are rebuilding our defenses. We have regained the confidence

and optimism about the future that have always been the real basis for our national strength. We see a new patriotism, a new pride in our country.

A lot of rethinking is going on about the Vietnam war—a lot of healthy rethinking. Many who bitterly opposed it have a more sober assessment now of the price that was paid for failure. Many who supported it have a more sober understanding now of the responsibilities that rest on our nation's leaders when they call on Americans to make such a sacrifice. We know that we must be prudent in our commitments. We know that we must be honest with ourselves about the costs that our exertions will exact. And we should have learned that we must maintain the ability to engage with, and support, those striving for freedom, so that options *other* than American military involvement remain open.

The Relevance of the Vietnam Experience

That experience has many other lessons. We acted under many illusions during the Vietnam period, which events since 1975 should have dispelled. We have no excuse for falling prey to the same illusions again.

During the Vietnam war, we heard an endless and shifting sequence of apologies for the communists: that they were "nationalists"; that they were an indigenous anticolonial movement; that they were engaged in a civil war that the outside world should not meddle in. As these arguments were proved hollow, the apologies changed. We heard that a communist victory would not have harmful consequences, either in their countries or the surrounding region. We were told that the communists' ambitions would be satisfied, that their behavior would become moderate. As these assertions became less convincing, the apologies turned to attack those who fought to be free of communism: our friends were denounced as corrupt and dictatorial, unworthy of our support. Their smallest misdeeds were magnified and condemned.

Then we heard the theme that we should not seek "military solutions," that such conflicts were the product of deep-seated economic and social factors. The answer, they said, was not security assistance but aid to develop the economy and raise living standards. But how do you address economic and social needs when communist guerrillas—as in Vietnam then and in Central America now—are waging war *against* the economy in order to maximize hardship? Our economic aid then, as now, is massive; but development must be built on the base of security. And what are the chances for diplomatic solutions if—as we saw after the 1973 Paris agreement—we fail to maintain the balance of strength on which successful negotiation depends? Escapism about the realities of power and security—that is a pretty good definition of isolationism.

And finally, of course, the critics turned their attack on America. America can do no right, they said. Now, criticism of policy is natural and commonplace in a democracy. But we should bear this past experience in mind in our contemporary debates. The litany of apology for communists, and condemnation for America and our friends, is beginning again. Can we afford to be naive again about the consequences when we pull back, about the special ruthlessness of communist rule? Do the American people really accept the notion that *we,* and our friends, are the representatives of evil?

The American people believe in their country and in its role as a force for good. They want to see an effective foreign policy that blocks aggression and advances the cause of freedom and democracy. They are tired of setbacks, especially those that result from restraints we impose on ourselves.

Vietnam and Central America

Vietnam and Central America—I want to tackle this analogy head-on.

Our goals in Central America *are* like those we had in Vietnam: democracy, economic progress, and security against aggression. In Central America, our policy of nurturing the forces of democracy with economic and military aid and social reform has been working—without American combat troops. And by virtue of simple geography, there can be no conceivable doubt that Central America is vital to our own security.

With the recent legislative and municipal elections. El Salvador has now held four free elections in the past 3 years. When the new assembly takes office shortly, El Salvador will have completed an extraordinary exercise in democracy—drafting a new constitution and electing a new government, all in the midst of a guerrilla war. The state of human rights is greatly improved, the rule of law is strengthened, and the performance of the armed forces markedly better. Americans can be proud of the progress of democracy in El Salvador and in Central America as a whole.

The key exception is Nicaragua. Just as the Vietnamese communists used progressive and nationalist slogans to conceal their intentions, the Nicaraguan communists employ slogans of social reform, nationalism, and democracy to obscure their totalitarian goals. The 1960 platform of the communists in South Vietnam promised:

Freedom of expression, press, assembly and association, travel, religion, and other democratic liberties will be promulgated. Religous, political, and patriotic organizations will be permitted freedom of activity regardless of belief and tendencies. There will be a general amnesty for all political detainees [and] the concentration camps dissolved. . . . [I]llegal arrests, illegal imprisonment, torture, and corporal punishment shall be forbidden.

These promises were repeated time after time. We find similar promises in the letter the Nicaraguan revolutionary junta sent to the Organization of American States in July 1979. The junta, which included the communist leader Daniel Ortega, declared its "firm intention to establish full observance of human rights" and to "call . . . free elections." The Nicaraguan communists made the same commitment when they agreed to the Contadora Document of Objectives in September 1983, and when they said they accepted the Contadora draft treaty of September 1984.

What the communists, in fact, have tried to do since they took power in Nicaragua is the opposite: to suppress or drive out noncommunist democratic political forces; to install an apparatus of state control down to the neighborhood level; to build a huge war machine; to repress the Roman Catholic Church; to persecute Indians and other ethnic groups, including forcible relocations of population; and to welcome thousands of Cuban, Soviet, East European, PLO [Palestine Liberation Organization], and Libyan military and civilian personnel. They have formed links with PLO, Iranian, and Libyan terrorists, and are testing their skills as drug traffickers. Like the Vietnamese communists, they have become a threat to their neighbors.

Broken promises; communist dictatorship; refugees; widened Soviet influence, this time near our very borders—here is your parallel between Vietnam and Central America.

Brave Nicaraguans—perhaps up to 15,000—are fighting to recover the promise of the 1979 revolution from the communists who betrayed it. They deserve our support. They are struggling to prevent the consolidation and expansion of communist power on our doorstep and to save the people of Nicaragua from the fate of the people of Cuba, South Vietnam, Cambodia, and Laos. Those who assure us that these dire consequences are *not* in prospect are some of those who assured us of the same in Indochina before 1975.

Particularly today, what can we as a country say to a young Nicaraguan: "Learn to live with oppression; only those of us who already have freedom deserve to pass it on to our children"? What can we say to those Salvadorans who stood so bravely in line to vote: "We may give you some aid for self-defense, but we will also give a free hand from a privileged sanctuary to the communists in Nicaragua to undermine your new democratic institutions"?

The critical issue today is whether the Nicaraguan communists will take up in good faith the call of the church and of the democratic opposition for a cease-fire and national dialogue. This is what President Reagan called for on April 4. What does it tell us about the Nicaraguan regime that it refuses dialogue combined with a cease-fire? What does it tell us about who is prolonging the killing? About who is the enemy of democracy? What does it tell us about the prospects for peace in Central America if the democratic forces are abandoned?

The ordeal of Indochina in the past decade—as well as the oppressions endured by the people of Cuba and every other country where communists have seized power—should teach us something. The experience of Iran since the fall of the Shah is also instructive. Do we want another Cuba in this hemisphere? How many times must we learn the same lesson, and what is America's responsibility?

America's Responsibility

Today, we remember a setback, but the noble cause of defending freedom is still our cause. Our friends and allies still rely on us. Our responsibility remains.

America's Armed Forces are still the bulwark of peace and security for the free world. America's diplomats are still on the front line of efforts to reduce arsenals, settle conflicts, and push back the danger of war.

The larger lesson of the past decade is that when America lost faith in itself, world stability suffered and freedom lost ground. This must never happen again. We carry the banner of liberty, democracy, the dignity of the individual, tolerance, the rule of law. Throughout our history, including the period of Vietnam, we have been the champion of freedom, a haven of opportunity, and a beacon of hope to oppressed peoples everywhere.

Let us be true to the hopes invested in us. Let us live up to our ideals and be their strong and faithful champion around the world.

BIBLIOGRAPHY

An asterisk (*) preceding a reference indicates that the article or part of it has been reprinted in this book.

Books and Pamphlets

Beidler, Philip D. American literature and the experience of Vietnam. University of Georgia Press. '82.

Berman, Larry. Planning a tragedy: the Americanization of the war in Vietnam. Norton. '82.

Dawson, Alan. 55 days: the fall of South Vietnam. Prentice Hall. '77.

Duiker, William J. Vietnam since the fall of Saigon. Ohio University Press. '81.

Emerson, Gloria. Winners and losers. Random House. '77.

FitzGerald, Frances. Fire in the lake: the Vietnamese and the Americans in Vietnam. Little, Brown, '72.

Hawthorn, Lesleyanne. Refugee: the Vietnam experience. Oxford University Press. '82.

Henkin, Alan B. Between two cultures: the Vietnamese in America. Century Twenty One. '81.

Herr, Michael. Dispatches. Knopf. '77.

Herring, George C. America's longest war: the United States and Vietnam, 1950–1975. Dodd, Mead, '78.

Karnow, Stanley. Vietnam: a history. Viking. '83.

Kendrick, Alexander. The wound within: America in the Vietnam years 1965–1974. Little, Brown. '75.

Lifton, Robert J. Home from the war: Vietnam veterans. Basic. '85.

MacPherson, Myra. Long time passing: Vietnam and the haunted generation. Doubleday. '84.

Podhoretz, Norman. Why we were in Vietnam. Simon & Schuster. '82.

Schandler, Herbert. Lyndon Johnson and Vietnam: the unmaking of a president. Princeton University Press. '77.

Surrey, David S. Choice of resistance: Vietnam era military and draft resisters in Canada. Praeger. '82.

Zaroulis, Nancy. Who spoke up? American protest against the war in Vietnam, 1963–1975. Doubleday. '84.

PERIODICALS

America. 148:54. Ja. 22, '83. The Vietnam war memorial. Thomas M. Gannon.

Atlantic. 255:71–82. Ja. '85. Vietnam's Vietnam. Stephen J. Morris.

Atlantic. 255:90–118. Ap. '85. The road to hill 10. William Broyles, Jr.

Christian Century. 102:442. My. 1, '85. Vietnam: widening our perspective. Stewart W. Herman.

Christian Science Monitor. p 24. S. 30, '82. Bringing America's children home. Editorial.

Christian Science Monitor. p 6. Je. 2, '83. Vietnam's 'camps'; dumping grounds for nonconformists.

Christian Science Monitor. p 6. N. 23, '83. U. S. continues search for soldiers still missing in Vietnam.

Christian Science Monitor. p 16. Ap. 3, '85. 10 years after. John Hughes.

Christian Science Monitor. p 16. Ap. 16, '85. Lessons from Vietnam. Joseph C. Harsch.

Christian Science Monitor. p 11. Ap. 29, '85. After the war, new regime silenced even supporters. Paul Quinn-Judge.

*Commentary. 73:52–53. F. '82. The scandal of Cambodia. Martin F. Herz.

Commentary. 74:39–47. S. '82. Vietnam under communism. Stephen J. Morris.

*Commentary. 77:35–41 Ap. '84. Vietnam: the revised standard version. Norman Podhoretz.

Commentary. 78:51–56. O. '84. Of arms, men and monuments. Tod Lindberg.

*Commonweal. 110:79–99. Jl. 15, '83. A wall for remembering. David A. Hoekema.

Commonweal. 110:646–47. D. 2, '83. Vietnam never ended. Steven Kramer.

*Commonweal. 112:441–42. Ag. 9, '85. A name for loss: memorials of Vietnam. Frank McConnell.

Current History. 83:409–12, 32–33. The legacy of history in Vietnam. William J. Duiker.

Daedalus. 111:157–67. Fall '82. Vietnam: the television war. Michael Mandelbaum.

Department of State Bulletin. 83:35–38. N. '83. Kampuchea after 5 years of Vietnamese occupation. John C. Monjo.

*Department of State Bulletin. 84:51–54. N. '84. Cambodia: the search for peace. Paul D. Wolfowitz.

*Department of State Bulletin. 85:57–58. Ja. '85. Situation in Kampu-
chea. Jeane J. Kirkpatrick.

*Department of State Bulletin. 85:13–16. Je. '85. The meaning of Viet-
nam. George P. Shultz.

Foreign Affairs. 63:722–46. Spring '85. What *are* the lessons of Vietnam?
David Fromkin and James Chace.

Foreign Affairs. 63:747–58. Spring '85. Coming to grips with Vietnam.
John Wheeler.

Harper's. 268:67–72. Je. '84. Barely suppressed screams. C. D. B. Bry-
an.

*Harper's. 270:35–46. Ap. '85. What are the consequences of Vietnam?
James Chace and others.

History Today. 34:45–48. O. '84. The Vietnam war. R. B. Smith.

Los Angeles Times. Sec. 1, p 12. D. 19, '82. Amerasian emigration may
stall despite new U. S. open door. Bob Sector.

Los Angeles Times. Sec. 1-B p 1. Je. 23, '83. Cambodian coalition completes year of its shaky life. Bob Sector.

Los Angeles Times. Sec. 1-A, p 1. Jl. 22, '83. 'Friendship pass' becomes
symbol of Sino-Vietnamese enmity. Michael Parks.

Los Angeles Times. Sec. 1, p 1. My. 28, '84. Vietnam losing economic
war; achieves revolutionary goals, fails to prosper. William Touhy.

Los Angeles Times. Sec. V, p 1. Je. 22, '85. PBS series on Vietnam draws
fire.

Maclean's. 98:40–42. Ap. 29, '85. A crippled nation. Marcus Gee.

Monthly Review. 37:14–21. Je. '85. A short history of the war in Vietnam. Jayne Werner.

Nation. 235:486. N. 13, '82. Minority report. Christopher Hitchens.

*Nation. 236:41–44. Ja. 15, '83. On the long road toward Phnom Penh.
Jacques Bekaert.

Nation. 237:570–73. D. 3, '83. A balance of error? Peter Biskind.

National Geographic. 167:555–73. To heal a nation. Joel L. Swerdlow.

National Review. 34:1213. O. 1, '82. Vietnam Gulag . . . and baby
makes three. Doan Van Toai.

National Review. 37:26–35, 40–42. My. 3, '85. Indochina revisited; the
demise of liberal internationalism. John P. Roche.

Nation's Business. 71:65–67. Je. '83. The high cost of helping. S. Kantor.

*New Republic. 187:6,39. D. 6, '82. What's in a name? Editorial.

*New Republic. 192:13–16. Ap. 29, '85. Why the war was immoral.
Hendrik Hertzberg.

New Republic. 192:17–19. Ap., '85. The empire's new clothes. Henry Fairlie.

New Republic. 192:20–23, Ap. 29, '85. How we lost. Harry G. Summers, Jr.

New Republic. 192:39–41. Ap. 29, '85. Still burning. Stephen Sestanovich.

*New Republic. 193:15,17–19. Jl. 1, '85. The myth of the lost POWs. James Rosenthal.

New York. 15:16. O. 25, '82. The Vietnam war that's still being fought.

New York Review of Books. 31:16. My. 1, '84. The burial of Cambodia. William Shawcross.

New York Review of Books. 32:50. My. 30, '85. Anniversaries. Murray Kempton.

New York Review of Books. 32:22. Je. 13, '85. Parade's end. Murray Kempton.

New York Review of Books. 32:38–40. Ag. 15, '85. Vietnam: casualties of peace. Gavin Young.

New York Times. p E23. Ja. 23, '83. Vietnam's 10 years of 'peace.' Tad Szalc.

New York Times. p 3. Mr. 25, '83. New group of children leave Vietnam.

New York Times. p 1. Ap. 18, '84. Amerasian war orphans come to U.S. Nan Robertson.

New York Times. p 1. Ap. 18, 85. 10 years after Vietnam, U. S. a power in Asia. Leslie H. Gelb.

New York Times. Sec. 4, p E23. Ap. 28, '85. Lessons of Vietnam. Anthony Lewis.

New York Times. P 1. S. 3, '85. Khmer Rouge in Cambodia says Pol Pot has retired as rebel chief. Barbara Crossette.

New York Times Book Review. 89:1. Ap. 15, '84. Novelists and Vietnam scholarship. Fox Butterfield.

*New York Times Magazine. 133:24–27, 54–63. O. 30, '83. A bitter peace: life in Vietnam. Craig R. Whitney.

New York Times Magazine. 134:60. Ja. 13, '85. Apocalypse continued. Edward Tick.

New York Times Magazine. 134:28–34. Mr. 31, '85. The enduring legacy. Joseph Lelyveld.

New York Times Magazine. 134:50–51, 54–57. Mr. 31, '85. The war and the arts: there has been a cultural turnaround on the subject of Vietnam. Samuel G. Freedman.

New Yorker. 61:35–36. Mr. 18, '85. Notes and comment.

New Yorker. Part I. 61:104–18+. Ap. 22, '85. Part II. 61:92–108+. Ap. 29, '85. Return to Vietnam. Richard Shaplen.

Newsweek. 100:78. O. 11, '82. Coming 'home' at last. James LeMoyne.

Newsweek. 100:80–81,86. N. 22, '82. Honoring Vietnam veterans—at last. Tom Morganthau.

Newsweek. 100:42. D. 6, '82. The newest immigrants. Martin Kasindorf.

Newsweek. 102:91–93. O. 10, '83. America's first television war. William Broyles, Jr.

Newsweek. 104:46. S. 24, '84. Amends for the left-behinds. Mark Whitaker.

*Newsweek. 105:30–39. Ap. 8, '85. 'Where is my father?' Melinda Beck.

Newsweek. 105:48. My. 13, '85. Vietnam's awkward drill; ten years after the fall of Saigon, hardships remain. Nancy Cooper.

Progressive. 47:28. N. '83. Again the television war. John Spragens, Jr.

Scholastic Update. 117:9–10. Mr. 29, '85. Vietnam today: still divided, still at war. Peter M. Jones.

Scholastic Update. 117:13–14. Mr. 29, '85. The children that America left behind. Colleen O'Brien.

Science News. 125:261. Ap. 28, '84. Vietnam vets: how well did they adjust? B. Bower.

Society. 21:4–17. N./D. '83. Defense without purpose. Harry G. Summers, Jr.

Society. 21:18–22. N./D. '83. Distorting history. Gareth Porter.

Society. 21:23–26. N./D. '83. Lessons yet to be learned. Thomas J. Bellows.

*Time. 120:44–46. N. 22, '82. A homecoming at last. Kurt Andersen.

Time. 121:82–85. Ap. 25, '83. When will peace begin? James Kelly.

Time. 124:44. N. 26, '84. Healing Viet Nam's wounds. Alessandra Stanley.

Time. 125:71. Ja. 7, '85. Dry-season rite; fresh fighting in Kampuchea. Mark Whitaker.

Time. 125:37. F. 25, '85. 'Greatest victory': the Khmer Rouge retreat as Hanoi overruns a key sanctuary. George Russell.

Time. 125:20–31. Ap. 15, '85. A bloody rite of passage. Lance Morrow.

Time. 125:47. Jl. 1, '85. Taking AIM again at Viet Nam. Richard Zoglin.

U. S. News & World Report. 94:14. F. 21, '83. Human rights score: gains and losses.

U. S. News & World Report. 95:25. Ag. 8, '83. At the scene: how guerrillas pin down a Soviet Ally.

U. S. News & World Report. 95:65. N. 21, '83. A memorial wall that • healed our wounds.

U. S. News & World Report. 98:25–27. Ja. 14, '85. As troubles mount for communist Vietnam. Robert Kaylor.

*U. S. News & World Report. 98:45–47. Ja. 21, '85. A decade after Saigon's fall, a painful peace. Robert Kaylor.

U. S. News & World Report. 98:39–40. Ap. 22, '85. Dominoes that did not fall. Robert Kaylor & Walter Taylor.

*U. S. News & World Report. 98:60–62. My. 6, '85. Hanoi still aches a decade after victory. Robert Kaylor.

*USA Today. 112:21–37. My. '84. Families of Vietnam War POW's and MIA's: the ordeal continues. Ann Martin.

Wall Street Journal. p 1. Ja. 14, '85. Vietnam's legacy: a decade after war, U. S. leaders still feel effects of the defeat. David Ignatius.

Wall Street Journal. p 1. Mr. 14, '85. Of the Asian dominoes that haven't fallen, several are thriving.

Wall Street Journal. p 1. Mr. 21, '85. Indochinese refugees adapt quickly in U. S., using survival skills.

Washington Post. p C1. Jl. 29, '84. Asia's 'dominoes' didn't fall after Vietnam, they got rich instead. Don Oberdorfer.

Washington Post. p. A1. Ap. 19, '85. Lessons of the past; a decade later, consensus elusive for scholars and students alike.

Washington Post. p A1. Ap. 21, '85. A decade of time lost; Hanoi continues calls for sacrifice, now seeks renewed ties with U. S. William Branigin.

Washington Post. p A1. Ap. 23, '85. Shotgun wedding; north's political rule is unchallenged, but south's cultural influence spreads. William Branigin.

Washington Post. p A1. Ap. 24, '85. Aging leadership; Ho Chi Minh's colleagues still rule in Hanoi. William Branigin.

World Press Review. 32:48+. Je. '85. Vietnam's anniversary battles. David Jenkins.

World Press Review. 32:48. Jl. '85. Rewriting history. John Pilger.

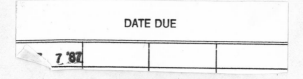